100% CAPACITY

The End of Gender Balance as We Know It

JENNIFER KENNY

100% CAPACITY

Cataloguing in publication information is
available from Library and Archives Canada.
ISBN 978-1-77458-357-9 (paperback)
ISBN 978-1-77458-358-6 (ebook)

Page Two
pagetwo.com

Edited by James Harbeck
Copyedited by Crissy Calhoun
Proofread by Alison Strobel
Cover design by Jennifer Lum
Interior design and illustrations by Cameron McKague
Printed and bound in Canada by Friesens
Distributed in Canada by Raincoast Books
Distributed in the US and internationally by Macmillan

24 25 26 27 28   5 4 3 2 1

jenniferkenny.com

*This book is in honor of all the women and men
who know who they are and have shown me the way.
For all the women and men who have attended my workshops,
allowed me to interview them, and joined
in discussion groups—validating my ideas, inspiring
me, giving me great stories, and helping me create
vibrant personas for this book.*

*This book is also for all of the women and men
who are determined to figure it out—I am right here
along with you, and I hope this is valuable for you in
your quest.*

Contents

Author's Note

THIS BOOK is the result of twenty years of inquiry, research, exploration, and conversation. I wrote it because I firmly believe that women lead differently. I've worked with men for most of my career, and I was very interested in finding a way for them to understand how women lead differently. I also believed that if women could articulate how they lead differently, we humans would be able to amplify each other and not only create exponentially more value but also deal with some of the biggest problems facing us today, while creating workplaces where we are seen, heard, and valued—and ultimately where gender becomes a nonissue.

On occasion, we all find ourselves at odds with the mores of the workplace. Whatever was supposed to be obvious feels bad, does not land, rubs us the wrong way, or seems inefficient. I wrote this book because I believe a lot of these moments of friction come from a lack of understanding difference and a lack of appreciation of unique value. This friction offers an undiscovered opportunity. There's richness in this tension. Difference of any sort and to any degree is part of how we recognize our own edges and prepare for growth. What otherwise might go unnoticed, and what we find ourselves naturally attuned to, is part of our unique value as individuals.

Over the course of my corporate career in consulting, leadership, and innovation, I have discovered that corporate environments struggle to integrate different kinds of leadership into their structures. At best, we watch our workplaces pander to, tokenize, or condescend to distinct flavors of leadership. Regardless of what environment I am working in, be it research, banking, energy, or technology, leadership that doesn't follow the established formula often gets neglected. We fumble in positioning and leveraging some of our best leaders. We don't know what to do with them.

This observation left me with some enduring questions. How can I create ideal structures so that leadership qualities, in all their variety, are used to fullest advantage? How do you do that while cultivating the leadership capabilities of the people on your team? How do you do that while allowing for a high degree of emergence and exploration, which is essential for both incremental and disruptive innovation? How do you do this inside corporations where this is not yet the norm?

If these are questions that you live with every day, then I wrote this book for you.

As a scientist and engineer, I have always balked at the idea that the dominant command-and-control approach to leadership and management was the most effective one, even though it seemed like the only one used to lead and manage teams of researchers, innovators, engineers, and scientists. I always felt that there had to be another and more effective way.

I know that sometimes differences can make our work complicated. And I also know that our uniqueness, when elevated to its best level, can offer incredible value. I've sought to put this approach together in a pragmatic and structured way that gives us tools, language, and narrative to chart our own course as we seek to bring a more innovative, robust, and valuable understanding of leadership to our workplaces and to deliver measurable and outstanding results that only something as powerful as 100% Capacity Leadership can offer.

I hope this book will benefit each person I have had the pleasure of working with over the years, as well as those I have yet to work with.

I'm delighted you are reading this book, and I hope you get a lot out of it. If you do, in the spirit of serving others, please pass it on.

In gratitude,
Jennifer

Introduction

The Power of Recognition

Iso E Super is a highly versatile odor molecule. It is in almost every synthetic fragrance available on today's market. Iso E Super is a novel molecule, initially synthesized by chemists John B. Hall and James M. Sanders for International Flavors & Fragrances in 1973. The molecule is to perfumery what monosodium glutamate (MSG) is to takeaway cuisine. It helps to improve the longevity of other notes in a given scent, extends the projection range of the scent, and brings out a clarity of notes, making them their most pungent.

In 1988, the world of perfumery saw a breakthrough when Dior's masculine fragrance Fahrenheit was launched. It used an overdose of Iso E Super. At the time, this was unusual, which allowed Dior to get away from the masculine scent clichés that dominated the 1980s' cologne market. They envisioned something new.

Today, the unique qualities of Iso E Super make the molecule remarkably popular in the production of scent. Most people would know its smell—if they had the chance to smell it in isolation. It's familiar, but it's difficult to put your finger on. It's in everything, but it remains hard to recognize. Unless you're in the know, you're likely to misattribute its pleasant aroma to something else in the product. In fact, one of the unique features of Iso E Super is that some people can't smell it easily. Because of the molecule's large size, it can be difficult to detect. This only amplifies the effect—our noses can sense that something is going on, but our noses don't seem to be clear about what exactly that is.

Most of us have learned, through our years at work, that recognition counts. Recognizing what's different is the first step, and having the language to describe it is the next. With clear recognition, you can stand out and get the help, funding, or involvement you need, rather than being overlooked and undervalued—and ultimately getting bypassed on next year's budget.

For many of us, however, recognition is partial. We're all doing things behind the scenes that can be easily, and often benevolently, overlooked. Just as Iso E Super blends into the background, we, too, can go unnoticed. Sometimes this is the reason work can be so exhausting. Maybe we know intimately how certain people, processes, and systems all work together. Maybe we are one of the few people who perceive the broad-scale impact of various strategic moves and decisions. Maybe not everyone on our team knows when to include an expert from another department and how to humbly ask them for help. And maybe none of these delicate skills receives the warranted recognition.

It's difficult to notice something you've never been taught to notice before. Most of us have had the experience of going to a restaurant, be it particularly fancy or serving an unfamiliar cuisine, and not knowing how to describe exactly what it is that we're tasting. This is where we are with gender balance in the workplace. And we're losing value as a result.

The Goal

First published in 1984, *The Goal: A Process of Ongoing Improvement* is a novel designed to transform management thinking. The book was groundbreaking upon its initial release and has been reissued three times in the decades since. Authors Eliyahu M. Goldratt and Jeff Cox make the point that "since the strength of the chain is determined by the weakest link, then the first step to improve an organization must be to identify the weakest link."

In this early part of the twenty-first century, it is clearer than ever that humans are not effectively leveraging our resources. We are acutely aware that our habitual disregard for resources does not serve us and, in fact, that we are placing ourselves in harm's way. And the biggest resource that we are not effectively using is 50% of who we, as the human race, are. We are not getting full value from feminine leadership. Our lack of understanding of our full leadership capacity is both our weakest link and our biggest opportunity when it comes to innovation and corporate performance.

Any CEO and/or executive team would be ecstatic if you told them you could generate a 2% year-over-year increase in earnings or could make their company 27% more likely to produce longer-term customer value. This is the scale of impact that gender-balanced teams can deliver. The data shows that corporations with gender-balanced leadership perform better on core financial and functional metrics. Gender-balanced leadership offers tangible value, and it's waiting to be realized.

Today, the largest ever generation of highly educated and financially aware women are getting restless. In countries or organizations where gender equality is legislated and equal treatment for women and girls is established, we are still seeing a big gap in how women are engaging with society and business. It's not that women are ineffective, but that we both view and render them so. In developed nations and in companies where gender equality is an integral part of the culture, and of the human resources standard operating procedures, women are still opting out, leaving C-level positions or declining promotions. We must ask ourselves: Why? And what can we do about it?

We know that forward-looking countries are legislating gender balance both on corporate boards and in political and economic leadership. We see innovative leaders boldly articulating their commitment to an emotional intelligence quotient (EQ), to more collaboration and greater cohesion on their teams. These early signs indicate that change is afoot. However, until now, gender equity has been addressed from the perspective of correcting a deficit.

This book hopes to broaden our understanding. Gender equity is not a lack that we make up for; it's an abundance of already plentiful resources, capabilities, and leadership qualities that we don't witness in full because we don't know how or where to look. Like Iso E Super in Fahrenheit, gender balance feels natural. It is pervasive but, at the same time, seemingly elusive. Once you've been made aware of it, you won't stop noticing it. It is familiar, literally under our noses, but it's difficult to put your finger on. It's in everything, but it remains hard to recognize.

What we currently recognize as leadership is only half of what humans are capable of. This fact is at the core of this book. After years of researching in the corporate field, interviewing hundreds, and facilitating countless workshops, I want to enable leaders, regardless of gender, who want to be seen, heard, and valued. It's time for innovation and operational leaders to understand why gender-balanced teams deliver measurably better results and value in many domains of business and society. And it's time for all leaders to learn how to take advantage of this value by integrating the full spectrum of human leadership capabilities—100% Capacity Leadership—into their businesses.

This book is about how to get full value from people. But this is not a book about men versus women. This is a book about how all of us are neglecting the feminine half, and how all of us can get full value from both the feminine and the masculine.

Feminine or masculine archetypes extend beyond conventional limitations regarding sex and gender. We each embody some combination of these various archetypes. Consider scholar Joseph Campbell and his work outlining the hero's journey. Campbell's work has become contentious in recent decades because of its glaring exclusion: leaving out women as protagonists. However, most of us can recognize the universality of the hero's journey. We can readily map these mythological milestones onto our own lives, irrespective of our gender identity.

Think of the masculine as part of a collective body of wisdom. Think of the feminine as an equal part of that same body of knowledge. They are comparable to yin and yang in Taoism: opposing forces bound together, in tension with each other, giving rise to each other, interacting to form a dynamic system in which the whole is greater than the sum of its parts. As Virginia Woolf wrote in *A Room of One's Own*, "In each of us two powers preside, one male, one female... The androgynous mind is resonant and porous... naturally creative, incandescent, and undivided."

Where Do We Start?

Maybe you find yourself concerned about the entrenched status quo of the corporate world. Maybe you feel like there is a growing chasm between established company leaders and the workforce, and leadership isn't structured in a way that allows for a shift in vision. It feels like your company's efforts to address gender balance have been ineffective—just pink-washing—and measuring stuff like employee engagement doesn't make change happen. Efforts to close the gap between established corporate logics have missed the opportunity to positively influence the real-life stakeholders. Is there anything on the horizon that can bridge this growing gap in an authentic and sustainable way?

Or perhaps you find yourself overloaded by the efforts to change the status quo, so much so that you lose interest and turn to indifference. Maybe relationships outside work offer you something healthy and dynamic, but you long ago stopped expecting that sort of emotional flexibility while at your job. You would love to form real, innovative partnerships with your coworkers, but you are resigned to the idea that the rudimentary connections you have work well enough for now. You work consciously to change what you can, but you accept what you can't seem to change; it's foolish to continue to rail against what is already in place using the same tools, mindset, strategy, and old rhetoric. And you know that this means that you are missing out at work—and so is the company you work for.

However, you also know that someone at your workplace does the unrecognized work of paying attention to how individuals in the company are connected—which dynamics are pertinent to navigating projects and completing large works—and who collaborates well. Someone you work with keeps a mental list and knows who responds well under pressure, who remains calm. Someone else you work with has figured out how to keep professional women, who so often feel undervalued or misunderstood, on their team. They personally have cracked the code. Unfortunately, no one has asked them what it is that they're doing differently or what practices they have implemented to keep women on their team. And many times, they themselves don't know—they are just doing it.

We all notice the relevance and the value of these abilities. It's the reason we might contact one particular coworker, and it's why we look to a specific team member for help when something tricky arises. However, while we might understand the specific and unique value within all of our coworkers, our companies often fail to leverage these abilities.

On an operational level, these sometimes-invisible abilities are what we innately have. Our skills are things we choose to teach ourselves and learn from others. Our competencies are the things we regularly focus on, and we use a combination of knowledge, ability, and skill to develop these competencies over time.

These competencies, or collective capacities, are what organizations aim to harness when they hire people for their skills. They hope that these skills and competencies will generate meaningful business results. However, right now, this is beyond what a firm is likely to receive when a new hire walks in the door. Great results are generated when you align individuals' competencies with structural practices designed to facilitate growth.

In this book, I will outline practices that ignite behaviors that support our own growth. By doing this, we will also be supporting the growth of others. We are helping our work world progress towards autonomy and ultimately towards community, mastery, and purpose. Over time, individuals, teams, and companies who sustain these progressive practices become aspirational, increasing their innovation and performance capacity.

To help tell the story of what's going on and what we can do about it, I'm going to introduce you to five people: Daria, Bob, Evelyn, Tim, and Vera. These are not real people—not exactly. They're personas based on real people I have known in the decades spent incubating the ideas in this book. They personify traits I want to talk about. I definitely see some of myself in each of them—their shortcomings as well as their graces—and I suspect you'll see some of yourself in them too. I will be talking about challenges they face, and I will draw amply on my own experience with companies that hired me to help them resolve these problems.

Over the past two decades, I have interviewed women and men, collected case studies, and developed a robust methodology for this approach. The purpose of this book is to immerse you in the conversation, to help you see this opportunity and the changes we need to make to take advantage of it—to see it through the eyes of the people, or personas, we imagine in these conversations. I will also show you how to create new stories about what is possible; establish new structures to support, amplify, and institutionalize this and new language to bring it to life; and realize corporate performance gains. This is 100% Capacity Leadership.

Healthy and Unhealthy Masculine and Feminine Leadership Traits

Throughout the book, I will use new distinctions. You may be already familiar with the language and the terms, but like the Iso E Super molecule, you may not have observed these traits and qualities in your coworkers. You did not know how to see, hear, or value them nor how to amplify each other's fabulous traits and qualities. These distinctions will help you build your capacity to see, hear, value, and leverage these powerful traits. I'm introducing them here so you can track them as I use them; as we move through the book, you'll gain more and more of a sense of their context and how they work. I will point out the use of these distinctions, particularly when talking about personas. You'll see them easily—they are in bronze ink.

You will note that I refer to them as *healthy* and *unhealthy*. Our environment contributes enormously to our physical health and well-being, and in fact, it produces strong feedback loops. Similarly, healthy and unhealthy masculine and feminine leadership traits are impacted and sometimes sustained by both the person and the environment in which they work. What I call *healthy* leadership traits and characteristics can create growth, not just for the company but for the individuals, teams, and departments; safe space, where people get to innovate, since we don't innovate effectively without trust; more autonomy, another prerequisite for innovation; and less control, which can positively impact individual growth, innovation, and engagement. *Unhealthy* leadership traits and qualities, however, can lead to distrust, victimization, blame, sandbagging, hiding mistakes, reduced innovation, poorer performance, low engagement, missed opportunities... and the list goes on. A thriving and healthy organization requires thriving and healthy leaders and employees. So, my distinction here is simple but useful. It says nothing about the physical health of the individual, or their gender, but refers to the environment they create around them.

I suggest that you read these now and then use them as a reference as I introduce you to the language of 100% Capacity in situ and in action throughout this book. As you become familiar with these and more 100% Capacity distinctions and vocabulary, you will develop your own ability to see, hear, value, and leverage both your own and others' 100% Capacity Leadership.

Distinctions of the Healthy Masculine with Supported Business Competencies

Generating: What do they CREATE in the world?
- **Safety:** Concern for physical safety
- **Security:** Securing possessions
- **Material well-being:** Providing in the human-made world
- **Shelter:** Structure

Practices: What are they recurrently DOING?
- **Acting:** Providing
- **Making things:** Establishing repetition
- **Setting up procedures:** Seeing patterns
- **Observing repeatable actions:** Problem-solving
- **Building, constructing:** Making things

Desires: What do they WANT?
- **Belonging:** Being included, being part of
- **Honoring:** Keeping agreements, fulfilling obligations, being dutiful
- **Accomplishment:** Getting stuff done
- **Logic:** Following a sequential, straight-line way of doing things
- **Predictability:** Planning for the outcome, anticipating issues

Being: How do they SHOW UP in the world?
- **In action:** Doing or planning to do
- **Providing:** Giving others what they need to act

- Protecting: Establishing and protecting what is ours
- Competing: Understanding where we are in the world relative to others

Essence: What can you rely on them to BE?
- Patient: Forgiving mistakes
- In action: Doing, acting, fixing
- Playful: Joyful, lighthearted, goofy
- Steadfast: Committed, loyal, in for the long haul
- Structure: Equality

Distinctions of the Healthy Feminine with Supported Business Competencies

Generating: What do they CREATE in the world?
- Beauty: Appreciation of the aesthetics
- Abundance: Creating containers, doing amazing things with very little
- Newness: Initiating new opportunities, novelty
- Balance: Risk and caution, compliance and flexibility, ethics and consequences

Practices: What are they recurrently DOING?
- Observing synchronicity: Quantum leaps
- Gratitude: Giving attribution
- Appreciation: Recognizing others, celebrating
- Stillness: Listening, enabling others to feel heard

Desires: What do they WANT?
- Harmony: Finding middle ground
- Context: Recognizing collateral impact
- Respect: Attending to protocol
- Inclusion: Involving others

Being: How do they SHOW UP in the world?
- Receiving: Accepting help
- Perceiving: Bringing to light the unseen, knowing who to ask
- Accepting: Asking for help, "parking your ego"
- Relating: Attending to how people are connected, connecting to others

Essence: What can you rely on them to BE?
- Strong: Standing up for beliefs
- Flexible: Agile, adaptable
- Still: Creating room for others
- Resilient: Keep trying
- Persistent: Don't give up easily
- Structure: Equality

Distinctions of the Unhealthy Masculine with Associated Business Incompetencies

Generating: What do they CREATE in the world?
- War: My way; I am right
- Aggression: I am right, and I am angry
- Greed: I want my share of the pie, and it must be bigger than everyone else's
- Scarcity: There is not enough for everyone (scorched earth)
- Hierarchy: Top dog

Practices: What are they recurrently DOING?
- Bullying: Intimidating others, doing and/or taking what I want without regard for others
- Controlling: Excessive bureaucracy
- Lying: Avoiding dishonor, avoiding getting caught
- Blaming: It is someone else's fault
- Being right: Always believing that I have all the answers
- Arrogance: What you have to say is of no interest to me; I am right

Desires: What do they WANT?
- Power: Power to do what I want, power over others
- Material wealth: Never enough, never satisfied
- Control: Everything is subject to what I want

Being: How do they SHOW UP in the world?
- Controlling: Causing others to do what I want
- In power over others: Deciding the future of others
- Winning, beating others: Proof of supremacy at any cost
- Hyper-acting: Always busy, advising others on what to do, mansplaining

Essence: What can you rely on them to BE?
- Dominant: I am in control
- Angry: I am not happy, and it is everyone else's fault
- Power over: I cannot operate without power over others
- Threatening: Generating fear
- Structure: Power over

Distinctions of the Unhealthy Feminine with Associated Business Incompetencies

Generating: What do they CREATE in the world?
- Anxiety: Paralyzed by what might go wrong
- Emptiness: Never enough
- Strife: Taking sides, stirring up trouble
- Ugliness: Always seeing what is lacking
- Overwhelm: Incapable of action, indecisive

Practices: What are they recurrently DOING?
- Complaining: Quick to point out problems
- Wailing: Lamenting unfixable problems
- Manipulating: Hiding real goals or ambitions
- Disparaging: Putting down others

Desires: What do they WANT?
- Attention: Me, me, me; it's all about me
- Stuff: Never enough, nver satisfied

Being: How do they SHOW UP in the world?
- Always giving: The only right way is my way
- Demanding: Impossible, unspoken standards (it is impossible to be successful around me)
- Apologizing: Sorry about everything
- Transacting: No consideration for others
- Unfeeling or hyper-feeling: No humor, joy, or celebration; or hypersensitive, always victimized, begrudging
- Prickly, defensive: It's always my fault

Essence: What can you rely on them to BE?
- Fragile: Thin-skinned, easily offended (people walk on eggshells around me)
- Weak: Can't make anything happen for myself
- Vitriolic: Quick to anger and rant
- Victimhood: It is always someone else's fault
- Structure: There is no core structure; there is only appropriated power over

This book is an invitation to explore and to play. I hope to encourage all latent curiosity. Together we will come to understand and embrace the many facets of leadership wisdom that lie unobserved and therefore untapped within each of us. As we expand what we observe and implement, we'll see that gender equity is not a deficit that we must compensate for. At the end of this book, it is my hope that you will have the clarity and confidence to accurately identify and leverage all that is available to us through gender balance.

1

Double Your Capacity

Meet Daria

Daria is the director of R&D at TelGen, a publicly traded telecommunications equipment manufacturer. Let's say Daria joined TelGen a decade ago. She was recruited directly from her PhD program at SoCalTech. Daria has her own ideas about success. For her, solving big problems has always felt more important than making moves up the corporate ladder. When she came back from her last parental leave, her VP asked if she would lead one of the large research teams. Daria was surprised but enthusiastically accepted. This position has given her fantastic exposure to a bigger technology set. She enjoys seeing the entire product stack that TelGen produces. She is able to present a strong case to the Technology Council, of which she is newly a member, and that helps Daria as well as her team because the council decides how research funding is allocated across the whole company. For Daria, that has meant more resources, more funding, and more people.

However, there is a drawback: because her technology is core to almost all of the newest products, she must work with six other tech leads on a continual basis. As a result, the communication requirement has expanded massively compared to her previous position. She has to keep the sales and marketing VPs updated on progress. The executive team also requires a monthly update from all the research directors.

Daria has discovered that she finds the sales and marketing angle fun, and it has enabled her to get some of her teams closer to the customer. However, the execs demand a totally standardized format—she has no option to add context—and when she presents her monthly update, they always hammer her with a streak of aggressive questions. She feels it's all about predictability and control. While she gets the need for predictability, she finds the control very demotivating.

She's noticed that some of the other research directors seem to deal with this a lot better, and she's asked some of them for advice on how she can do a better job of getting her point across. While some of them have been really supportive, all their guidance has been about stuff like "preparing for battle" and having pre-meetings with her team to ask her every possible question and challenge her responses. She tried this, but it got out of hand, and she felt the message was getting completely lost, and everyone was just posturing and trying to be right.

At this point, she's started to think about leaving. When she catches herself in that thought, though, it really surprises her—if someone had asked her to describe her ideal job when she was completing her PhD, this would tick every box. She's not sure what she would look for in a new position, except not this, whatever *this* actually is. She's a scientist, an engineer, and she's profoundly disillusioned by how much she feels that, in this situation, those skills don't seem to be enough. There are things that everyone seems to expect, as if it's all common sense, but they don't make sense to her. It's not that she doesn't understand them; she just doesn't see the purpose and value.

Common Sense

In 1986, Fernando Flores introduced me to the powerful concept of common sense, which he defined as "the unspoken, unobserved frame of reference from which we all operate, interpret the world, learn, and engage with each other and with our customers." I was in my twenties at the time, and this revelation was earth-shattering. It reminds me of the moment you realize your own parents are fallible adults, same as anyone else. Without understanding the collective common sense and being able to differentiate it from our own specific viewpoint, we are unconscious of where our interpretations come from. And we spend all day, every day, acting on those interpretations. They trip us up. Often, they don't serve us. And we have never been trained to observe them. So what was the point of all those degrees? Really?

Understanding common sense is one of these wonderful paradigm-shifting realizations. Once you have learned it, you can't unlearn it. You are out in the world, and the sun is glaring down, exposing things you hadn't spotted before. Today I know that one of the core competencies of leadership that seeks to transform is the ability to help others see their own common sense. To help them see how that common sense is serving or undermining their efforts, supporting or detracting from their goals.

In the mid-'90s, I built a successful and lucrative business doing exactly that: helping people in corporations change their common sense about seemingly intractable problems such as supply chain partnerships, timely new product introduction, and trust-building with customers. I called it *process redesign*, because that was more acceptable to the common sense of business at the time—but it was truly about helping individuals, teams, and companies see how their common sense was supporting or hurting their articulation and implementation of their strategy, as well as helping them realize innovation and/or market opportunities.

So how does one go about seeing common sense? I have just quoted the definition of it as "the unspoken, unobserved frame of reference from which we all operate, interpret the world, learn, and engage with each other and with our customers." If it is unspoken and unobserved, where do we begin? We begin by looking at it and talking about it.

One dominant common sense belief is that masculinity is unfeeling, ruthless, and rooted in self-serving ambition. This understanding conflates being a bully with being a leader, and it stokes competition and undermines collaboration. Naturally, when we have a complex and compassionate understanding of the other individuals around us, we know this not to be true. The masculine, masculinity, and those who embody it are far more complex than this interpretation allows for. At worst, this model erodes trust and silences disagreement.

This definition of masculinity is an outdated cultural relic. It's not fixed in stone or hardwired in biology, no matter what some more traditional thinkers may claim. These are a set of learned behaviors, perpetuated by the small group who benefit from this kind of dated rigidity. What's learned can be unlearned. We can work to nurture leaders who empower and encourage. Leaders who understand how to enable all of their team members to excel and how to cultivate a workplace that thrives on co-invention, rewards innovation, values listening, and acknowledges the benefit of accepting diverse people and varied viewpoints, knowing that they bring fresh perspectives, essential skills, and new paradigms.

Similarly, our common sense ideas about the feminine, or how women show up at work and lead, are also superficial and seem to conflate women's leadership with soft skills and intuition—as if we have nothing more to bring to the party than how we feel. While bringing human feeling back into the workplace can be a good, even great, thing, this common sense belief about how women lead and what they contribute is overly simplistic. It misses the hugely important elements of understanding, seeing, and designing for interconnectedness; leveraging deep perception to assess situations; and making more effective decisions for the good of the people and the business.

Our common sense ideas about what's masculine and what's feminine, and about what leadership is and isn't, have left our workplace leadership very unbalanced. Taking things in rigid gendered terms can narrow our perspective. This book is about seeing the truth and seeing how to fix the problem. But why bother? Why is this a problem to fix? Because we're leaving enormous value on the table and enormous capacity unmined.

New Value: The Big 7

The leadership traits and qualities that get left on the table have the capacity to catalyze and, in partnership, realize solutions for some of our biggest problems and opportunities in business today. I refer to these as the Big 7, because they are seven of the biggest levers of exceptional corporate performance. There is ample data to support this incredible impact—if you know how to leverage it. Here are the Big 7 and how firms that lead on gender balance enjoy measurably superior performance on each.

1 Innovation: 76% more likely to get innovative ideas to market

2 Decision-making: Better decisions 73% of the time, and twice as quickly

3 Risk management: 24% fewer governance controversies per US$B in market cap

4 Customer experience: 27% more likely to create longer-term customer value

5 Employee engagement: 18% higher levels of team commitment

6 Operational excellence: Two additional percentage points of earnings before interest, taxes, depreciation, and amortization (EBITDA)

7 Strategy: 70% more likely to successfully identify and capture new markets

The more perspectives we have, the more we can co-create and innovate—if we know how—and yet the dominant voices have for a long time been too similar to one another. Gender balance is a key example of this. Evidence shows that gender equity and a diversity of gender drive innovation. This comes with financial incentives. To quote an article from EY, a global management consulting firm, "Boards with at least 30% women have higher profit margins than those who don't—we now see increasing evidence linking diversity to innovation, which is critical to successfully navigating disruption in this transformation age." But there is also a more invisible component. If we're hoping for stellar innovation, this kind of diversity can lead to innovation through avenues that we don't even expect.

What is it about gender balance that facilitates innovation? Research done by EY confirms that it is the diversity of views: "Innovation that uncovers new paths to growth will only spring from high-performing, gender-diverse teams that maximize the power of different opinions, perspectives and cultural references." This research reminds us that a difference of perspective is part of what drives creativity. Different opinions and perspectives push us in new directions. Diversity can spark innovation. If we are seeking the kind of newness that comes from delivering innovation, gender diversity is one ingredient to get us there. As noted in *Winning the War for Talent in Emerging Markets*, "A study by the Center for Talent Innovation found that companies with gender balanced teams are 70% more likely to capture new markets and 75% more likely to get innovative ideas to market. Evidence also suggests diversity leads to improved outcomes." I refer to this as leveraging the genius of gender balance. It's waiting there for us to see, hear, and leverage it. Let's explore the Big 7 in detail.

1. Innovation

Gender-diverse teams are 76% more likely to get innovative ideas to market. It follows that they are also more likely to generate and pursue new ideas. Inclusive cultures that foster collaboration and open communication are undoubtedly more conducive to innovation. Women are often underrepresented in leadership positions and in the fields of science, technology, engineering, and math (STEM), which can limit their ability to contribute to and drive innovation. We know women excel at **synthesis**, which would benefit STEM fields— more on this in chapter 3. We also know that diversity is a key driver of innovation and that promoting gender diversity in the workplace can help to create a more innovative and successful organization. Firms in the top quartile for gender diversity in upper management had a 66% higher return on investments than firms in the bottom quartile.

2. Decision-Making

Companies with gender-diverse leaders and teams make better decisions 73% of the time, and twice as quickly. Gender-balanced teams bring a wider range of perspectives and experiences to the table, which leads to more thorough and accurate problem-solving. The better **perception** offered by women in leadership begets a greater ability to iden-tify and address potential challenges. Women are more likely to seek out additional information before making a decision. This demonstrates their propensity for **inclu-sion,** as well as their awareness of **interconnectedness.** Research has shown companies helmed by women leaders tend to outperform others, particularly when it comes to decision-making. Women are more likely to engage in col-laborative decision-making processes that result in better performance. Women use "cooperation, collaboration and consensus-building more often—and more effectively—in order to make sound decisions." Although decisions made by women leaders result in better company-wide outcomes, men were found to be more confident in their decision-making abilities than women. Overall, we can see how lever-aging 100% Capacity Leadership in the workplace can create a more dynamic and innovative environment that leads to better decision-making and improved business outcomes.

3. Risk Management

Gender diversity on boards was correlated with stronger corporate governance practices. Balanced teams created 24% fewer governance controversies per market cap. In particular, the presence of women on boards was associated with more effective monitoring of management and a greater focus on long-term strategy. One study found that firms with gender-diverse boards had a 25% lower probability of incurring large financial losses due to lower operational risk. Striving for balance, the result of feminine leadership, leads to lower operational risk. Similarly, firms with gender-diverse boards have a higher probability of adopting international financial reporting standards and a higher likelihood of corporate governance compliance. This is demonstrative of **respect** and **integration**, both healthy feminine qualities.

Having women on the board can bring a range of benefits to a company, including improved financial performance, better corporate governance, and a greater focus on risk management and innovation. This highlights the importance of promoting gender diversity in the boardroom. A gender-balanced emphasis on **context** and **harmony** creates more successful and sustainable organizations.

Companies with higher levels of gender diversity on their boards have better financial performance, as measured by return on equity (ROE) and return on invested capital (ROIC). This relationship was particularly strong for companies in the bottom quartile of ROE and ROIC, which saw the greatest improvement in performance when they increased gender diversity on their boards.

4. Customer Experience

Gender-balanced workplaces are 27% more likely to create longer-term value. Diverse leadership teams may be more attuned to the needs and preferences of a diverse customer base. They are better able to develop and deliver products and services that appeal to a wide range of customers. This can lead to improved customer satisfaction and loyalty and can ultimately drive business success. Companies with three or more women in senior management scored higher in customer satisfaction, with a 5.3% increase over the average company. Here, we can see flexibility and skilled listening (**relating**) at play. Delivering additional value for a customer requires taking the time to listen deliberately to their concerns—something healthy feminine leadership is more likely to engage in. Overall, 100% Capacity Leadership can bring a range of benefits to companies, including improved financial performance, increased innovation, and enhanced customer experience. This highlights the importance of establishing 100% Capacity Leadership in the workplace, and it can help create more successful and sustainable organizations.

5. Employee Engagement

Gender-balanced teams have an 18% higher level of team commitment. When it comes to employee engagement, women are like a big lever to pull (**inclusion**). Engaged women in manager and director positions increase overall employee engagement by up to six percentage points, improving productivity and profit. One study found that gender diversity was positively related to team performance. Another study found that gender diversity was positively related to team decision quality. Research has also found that gender diversity is positively related to team cohesion. Our best "engagers" are often stuck engaging—and burn out because they are taking care of everyone else (managing) and not getting recognized for engaging. Research finds that gender diversity is associated with increased employee engagement, which in turn is correlated with better performance outcomes. Once we begin to actively engage the engagers and recognize and reward them for bringing that 100% Capacity Leadership quality to bear, we position our teams to amplify and enhance the capability of each player. This further increases our potential successful impact on the Big 7 or on whichever particular performance metric we have chosen to focus on.

6. Operational Excellence

Gender-balanced teams score two additional percentage points on EBITDA. As noted, companies with more diverse leadership teams, including a higher representation of women, tend to have better financial performance, as measured by higher returns on equity and higher profitability. This relationship is particularly strong for companies in the bottom quartile of financial performance, which saw the greatest improvement when they increased gender diversity on their leadership teams. Diverse leadership teams may be more attuned to the needs and preferences of a diverse customer base and may be better able to develop and deliver products and services that appeal to a wide range of customers (**flexibility**). This can lead to improved customer satisfaction and loyalty and can ultimately drive business success. In addition to the benefits for customer experience, diverse leadership teams tend to be more innovative and have higher levels of employee satisfaction. This can lead to improvements in operational excellence, as diverse teams may be better equipped to identify and address challenges and may be more motivated and engaged in their work (**synchronicity**). Promoting gender balance in the workplace can have a range of other benefits, including attracting and retaining top talent, and enhancing a company's reputation and brand image. Women in leadership positions can bring a range of benefits to companies, including improved financial performance, enhanced customer experience, increased innovation, higher levels of employee satisfaction, and improved operational excellence.

7. Strategy

Gender-diverse companies tend to be more innovative and have a stronger focus on long-term sustainability. They're also 70% more likely to successfully identify and capture new markets. Diverse teams may be better equipped to tackle challenges and come up with creative solutions. As mentioned, diverse leadership teams may be more attuned to the needs and preferences of a diverse customer base (**flexibility**), which can lead to improved customer satisfaction and loyalty. The Peterson Institute for International Economics found that companies with more women in top management positions had a 34% higher return on equity and a 53% higher return on invested capital. To us, this should demonstrate a stronger and more successful strategy (**resilience**) than teams lacking gender balance.

From Traditional to 100% Capacity Workplace

Let's begin to imagine what it would be like to work in an organization that could capitalize on these tremendous opportunities. That workplace would be focused on realizing the value of 100% of our human capacity. You can see the effects in the From Traditional to 100% Capacity Workplace table, which shows the shift from the traditional workplace model to one infused with 100% Capacity Leadership.

Traditional Workplace		100% Capacity Leadership
100 years of doing the same thing and expecting different results	→	Realizing the value of 100% of our capacity
Everyone assessed by how 50% contribute	→	Assessing everyone on what we all contribute
Individual women seen as amazing	→	Understanding the traits, qualities, and styles of masculine and feminine leaders
Gender balance stuck at 30%	→	Changing the game, not just moving the needle
Unconscious bias training	→	Understanding how to realize value
Blame and shame	→	Amplifying value
Everyone leading the same way	→	Seeing leadership as a spectrum between masculine and feminine
Untapped innovation capacity	→	Designing teams for increased innovation capacity
Untapped interdisciplinary opportunities	→	Innovating at the interdisciplinary margins

It's time to move beyond looking at the structures that might create small improvements (e.g., pay equity, striving for "gender blindness," new policies, etc.). Let's not just move the needle. Let's change the game! My previous book was *The Innovation Mindset*. Here in *100% Capacity* I want to introduce you to *how* mindsets get built. Traditionally, women have focused on creating structures that support women leaders, but the story we have told about the value of women's leadership has left us stuck. To move forward, we need to understand how change happens. We can systematically change our own mindsets, and other people's, by consciously changing our speech, structure, and story.

Speech

Speech gives us the distinctions that allow us to name, notice, and discuss things—to share realities between minds. Remember seeing your first Mini Cooper? The Mini Cooper was introduced into the United States in 2002. If you are not a car person, a small car is a small car like all other small cars. But I was in Palo Alto one evening and my friend pointed out (distinguished) the Mini Cooper to me. He went on and on about the origins, the paint, the charm, the speed, the engine, etc. Well, for the next few weeks, I saw the damn things everywhere! It is not as if everyone in San Francisco and the Peninsula had suddenly gone out and bought a Mini Cooper, but I now had the *distinction* "Mini Cooper" in my consciousness, so I *noticed* them everywhere. This is known as the frequency illusion, or Baader-Meinhof phenomenon.

Distinctions are powerful. They contain within them expertise, common sense, and wisdom. Distinctions have a way of pointing to what we are interested in observing. A distinction could be a word, phrase, picture, cartoon, or logo. Whatever form it takes, we are using a distinction to point out something that we want others to see and that we want to observe. We develop a wider and more expansive way of discussing the things that are relevant to us, and this vocabulary allows us to more accurately communicate with those who share our concerns. This is why it is so fun when we run across a stranger who knows just as much about opera or fermentation or Monty Python as we do! We have shared language.

This is a deeply human proclivity. If we are to bring in a new understanding of how humanity leads, we need new language to talk about the full spectrum of leadership. These are the tools we use to dig into the gold mine of 100% Capacity Leadership: the traits of healthy and unhealthy masculine and feminine leadership that I presented in the introduction and am highlighting in **bronze ink** throughout the book.

Structure

Structure is how our understanding of value is put into action and institutionalized in our company, community, or society— for example, conferences, tribes, training, learning communities, groups, communities of purpose, professional bodies, associations, and platforms. Anything that gathers us together or engages us with an institution can constitute structure. It's the shafts and lifts and trolleys in the gold mine. Sometimes these structures are the best way to disseminate ideas, make change, or spread information.

Magnet and Charter schools in America have embraced mindfulness and meditation, which is a good example of how structures can be used to shift and develop value. Recently, the progressive practice of meditation has been integrated into some public schools as well. Because research indicates there are positive benefits of mindfulness and meditation, the idea to offer these benefits to children emerged. Engaging in the secular process of observing thoughts and sitting still has benefits for developing minds. Until recently, the practice of meditation seemed far too niche, far too woo-woo for schools to consider. Here, we see an example of how structure can both shift and add value as it makes room for change. In this example, structure is being used to carry out a shared value.

Story

Story is what we tell ourselves and others about why the change we want is valuable or necessary. It's the map telling us where the gold is and how to mine it, and it's the market reports on the value of the gold we mine. Story is very important, because it defines roles for people and why they should care. Before we try to make change in an organization, it's critical that we listen to what matters to people and communicate to them why the change will matter to them.

There's a popular story about the early twentieth-century Antarctic explorer Ernest Shackleton. The story goes that he took out a short advertisement in the London *Times*:

> MEN WANTED for hazardous journey, small wages, bitter cold, long months of complete darkness, constant danger, safe return doubtful, honour and recognition in case of success.

Although historians doubt whether Shackleton himself took out the advertisement, the narrative is an inspiring one: five thousand people applied! Ultimately twenty-eight men (one of whom was a stowaway, so compelling was the narrative) and sixty-nine dogs went on the 1914 expedition with Shackleton.

The modern workplace carries with it a much lower chance of icy death (although some of us may relate to "long months of complete darkness"), but Shackleton has a lot to teach us about living in a state of courageous discomfort. He pursued discontinuous innovation and also relied on iterative innovation. On the one hand, Shackleton was part of the Heroic Age of Antarctic Exploration—he was not the first to explore the Antarctic, and he learned from those before him. On the other hand, his mission of completing the first crossing of the continent was not attempted again until 1958, forty-four years later. In this respect, he exemplifies discontinuous innovation. And he exemplified both types of innovation in his desire to explore the unexplored for the sake of humanity.

This is a powerful and compelling example of narrative or story. It taps into the energy and interests of the day. And it clearly invites people to join a movement, a change, something exciting that could make their lives and the lives of others better.

Our current gender-balance story is about a scarcity-based zero-sum game. It's all about us competing with each other and opposing each other—and that's destined for failure. We need to change the narrative if we are to see and act on the value that women's leadership brings. To speak about the value of women's leadership requires recognizing, identifying, and acknowledging the different components that men and women bring to leadership—changing our speech. The acts of listening and recognizing empower women. And quantifying and measuring what value women's leadership brings—to corporate profits, ROI, GDP, the Wellness Index—speaks in terms both women and men have been trained to use in evaluation. When we focus on value, we move into a space where both sides are working towards mutually beneficial results. From here, we can change the structures of our work institutions. And as we deliver mutually beneficial results, we will see that we have effectively changed the story about what is possible, and that lets us see our way to the next step: changing the game.

Daria Doesn't Want to Just Get By

A lot of masculine energy focuses on doing and on **action**. While this is a really necessary component of leadership, without a complementary being or **perception** focus (more detail on both in coming chapters), the absolutely critical functions of innovation, strategy, and listening get swept aside. Work becomes one very long and tiresome list of actions that are verified, checked, and contested in endless meetings. In many situations, the recommended best way to deal with this is to embrace it, but for people who are motivated more by the opportunity to listen, invent, and solve big problems, doing so creates an extraordinary level of discomfort. Let's spend some time designing a solution that will deliver better results for everyone and, most particularly, Daria, whom we introduced earlier.

Like all of the five personas in this book, Daria is an amalgamation of many people I've encountered in my career, both men and women. My brother talks about his experience of this kind of behavior—let's call it the "most senior = most right" paradigm. As he worked in a senior sales leadership role in a large multinational corporation, one with a very significant gender pay gap and minimal female representation at senior levels, the prevailing behavior he witnessed was very similar to that witnessed by Daria. The healthy masculine characteristics of generating **material well-being** and seeking **predictability** were there, but the overpowering values were the unhealthy masculine ones such as **aggression, being right**, and **scarcity**.

With clients in this type of environment, I walk them through a solution that involves looking outside of themselves, seeing the impact of various behaviors, and making a collective decision to embrace the one that's going to help them achieve their goals. Let's use Daria's company as a fictionalized example of how this unfolds.

The CFO of Daria's company brought us in. As CFO and also head of diversity, equity, and inclusion (DEI), she was responsible for an unusual but exceptionally powerful combination of hard measurable results, and she had a deep understanding of the latent value of diversity. She knew how to make valuable offers to the engineering divisions: "You don't need to lose your amazing female engineers, you can support your entire teams in establishing more effective cross-disciplinary innovation (the holy grail of innovation!), and you can positively impact your New Product Introduction and Tech Transfer cycle times and value impact. Which, by the way, you are measured on." Compelling!

We started by running a working session for the senior team. In these cases, we tend to jump straight to the distinctions and value. Then they can see how to leverage the distinctions immediately, which show up as tools to be used to generate value and reduce the noise-to-signal ratio. In other words, they get rid of friction, tension, and backchannels. They got it. And they got the 100% Capacity Leadership Compass, which I will introduce in chapter 3.

We followed this with an introduction to 100% Capacity Leadership for the directors and then immediately applied it via some design work with them. They all had ideas on how to make the process more supportive of innovation as well as more effective. Then we brought the directors together with the senior team and rolled up our sleeves. The outcome was:

- Daria stayed, as did eight other women in various teams who saw Daria as a role model.

- The cycle time for the review and reporting process was reduced by 30%—more time for research, engineering, and technology transfer.

- At the end of the year, the group had the highest number of pitched and funded projects within the company.

- In addition, their Tech Transfer success metrics went up by 20%.

2

Gender Balance Has Business Value

Meet Bob

Bob is the RVP of sales for commercial lending at a twenty-billion-dollar bank. His team consists of 250 agricultural commercial lenders. His work is all about results, quotas, and making his numbers (**material well-being**). He has strong long-term relationships with most of his customers and loves to golf and smoke cigars with them. He has no time for "fluff," as he puts it. The majority of his team are great guys, many of whom have worked for him for over a decade. He's hired some women, and they do a good job, but they can be a bit hard to manage. One of the areas where they excel is really understanding the customers and building trust with them. He believes this is because most of the women he brings on to his teams come from customer service backgrounds, and they get the details better than the guys (**logic and predictability**).

Many of Bob's customers are very traditional in their approach—they're ranchers and farmers—and when he's gone on meetings with some of the women, it's fascinating to see how differently they respond to a woman lender. It's all in the details, and for this reason he's given some of the largest accounts to a few of the leading women on his team, and the results have been impressively consistent.

Some of the women have encouraged others to come on board, and hey, he has no problem with that, but he worries that he'll end up with too many women on some of his teams. Another worrying trend has shown up, though: a few of the first-hired women have started to move on to other banks, and one of them took an account with her. He's asked a few of them what he could do to hold on to them, even offered them a raise, but he can't understand what's not working, and the girls in HR don't seem to have a clue either. He's done a few Google searches on why women leave good jobs, but it's not making a lot of sense to him. So while he's fine to hire more, he needs to manage that risk. He's got a strong pipeline of really qualified and motivated people who want to join his organization, and he's absolutely smashing his quotas. At the next RVP quarterly Team Gold Top Achievers event, he's going to really enjoy highlighting just how much success he's generated (**winning/beating others**).

Why Is Bob Part of the Problem?

I'm confident that the majority of the Western world's working population has encountered a Bob. They can be very constructive and effective leaders, demonstrating positive masculine leadership characteristics such as **setting up procedures, honoring**, and **protecting**, and in situations where not too much change happens, they can pretty consistently deliver success. The problem arises when more is required, and the same old, same old no longer cuts it. In competitive situations, their **scarcity** mindset can push them to double down on more unhealthy masculine characteristics, like **power over**.

However, one of the things the Bobs of this world are missing is that gender balance isn't just the *what*, it's the *how*. If Bob wants to build on his success, he has to take the critical step of moving beyond the "nice to have" social justice thinking to a mindset where the business value of gender balance is understood. What we will identify and learn in this chapter is exactly how we can demonstrate that in a way that appeals to everyone, including Bob.

Why Are We Still Stuck?

As I noted in chapter 1, corporations with gender-balanced leadership perform better on core financial and functional metrics, but globally firms bounce around below the 30% mark for women in leadership. There is growing pressure on organizations to make progress in this area. Billions of dollars have been invested, and laws passed, to improve gender balance in corporations. But despite serious and focused efforts, the gains have been achingly slow.

OECD data shows that female representation in senior corporate leadership has grown at slightly less than 1% per year for the last twelve years. In 2020, fewer than 30% of global senior management roles were held by women. That number drops to 11% for line management positions. In 2020, women holding corporate directorships among the 2,907 companies in the MSCI world index grew by only 0.6% (to 20.6%). That same year, just 2% of global start-up funding went to all-female founders, while 89% went to all-male start-up teams. And yet evidence indicates that start-ups with at least one female founder produce twice the revenues and profits.

Current efforts on gender balance primarily use diagnose-and-fix logic. Leadership classes teach women what keeps them from breaking through the glass ceiling. Unconscious bias training attempts to teach people to see past blind spots to become more inclusive. The success—or lack thereof—of these efforts has led us to this high-pressure moment where we know we are stuck. In 2020, the World Economic Forum found that achieving parity for men and women on the Economic Participation and Opportunity Index will take 257 years at the current rate of change.

We know that gender-balanced leadership offers tangible value, and it's waiting to be realized. So why aren't firms rushing in to reap the rewards? Why are we seemingly unable to take advantage of a well-documented and data-validated competitive advantage?

It can't be because we don't want to. CEOs and boards recognize it as both a financial and a market imperative. It's not for lack of pressure. Thomson Reuters maintains and publishes a Diversity and Inclusion Index to assess the practices of more than five thousand publicly traded companies globally. In 2020, Mercer reported on a survey of more than 1,150 companies that showed 66% were feeling pressure from their boards to make diversity and inclusion improvements. It's not because we haven't tried. As early as 2003, MIT professor Thomas Kochan estimated that firms were spending eight billion dollars a year on diversity efforts in the United States alone.

We can't seem to figure out what kind of a problem we need to fix. Is it . . .

A Women's Problem?

We thought it was a women's problem, so we took a social justice approach.

Of course, women deserve to be treated equally to men and given the same opportunities and pay, but while legislation supports women's equality, we desperately need a new story.

When it comes to gender equity, the social justice narrative can be heard by those in power as a zero-sum game. It attracts animosity and creates friction, which undermines the purpose of the work.

A Policy Problem?

We thought it was a policy problem, so we tweaked existing policies.

Realizing the business value of women's leadership and workforce participation, a growing number of companies have implemented policies such as extended family leave, personal time off, flexible work hours, and job sharing.

These operational fixes have had no discernable effect on female workforce participation rates and failed to prevent the exodus of women from the workplace during the COVID-19 pandemic. In the United States, Vice President Kamala Harris declared this situation a national emergency.

Policies have not prevented consistently high turnover among women, especially in senior positions where hires are more expensive and difficult to replace.

An Equity Problem?

We thought it was an equity problem, so we tried to treat women and men the same.

The notion of gender blindness is compelling to those who desire to be treated equally and have equal opportunity. This story has sincere and honest roots, but it is naive since it fails to take advantage of how women lead differently.

Operational fixes are considered the price of entry for attracting and retaining women, but they are not enough.

They do not address the fundamental issue of recognizing and paying women for the value they bring to corporations. Nor do the fixes help organizations actualize the full worth of women leaders.

A Lean-In Problem?

We thought it was a lean-in problem, so we developed women's leadership programs.

As the nondominant group, women have adapted in order to be recognized and rewarded by the dominant group. Women's leadership training often focuses on building familiar masculine leadership traits in women who are counseled to grow more confident in their abilities, lean in and take decisive action, and negotiate their way to higher positions. The unspoken headline is that women are somehow deficient and less equipped for success without special training. We are silent about the unique value of women's leadership as its own discipline.

When evaluated exclusively against masculine attributes and success criteria, women will be found lacking, simply because they are not men. Pushing hard to emulate men penalizes women's reputations. Their demeanor is perceived as inauthentic, because it is. In the current system, women are faced with a catch-22.

A Pipeline Problem?

We thought it was a pipeline problem, so we grew the female talent pipeline.

But evaluating 100% of employees through masculine leadership attributes *creates* the pipeline problem. The lens of masculine leadership means there will never be enough qualified women. Even when women achieve outstanding results (and they do), their methods are not well understood. This can make promoting them seem riskier than a male counterpart whose work style is familiar and therefore seems safe.

Corporations have invested billions of dollars in programs designed to generate a talent pool of women who fit into recognizable masculine norms. Despite these efforts, as noted, female representation in senior corporate leadership has increased by less than 1% per year for the last ten years.

Based on these interpretations of the problem(s), our solutions are not producing the results we seek. And so we are realizing the problem is really none of the above.

My research points to us being stuck because we don't know what women's leadership is. Through more than thirty years as a C-level executive, consultant to the Fortune 100, design and systems thinker, tech CEO and founder, and master of innovation practices, I've realized that breaking through the current logjam requires less focus on what is wrong—what the problem is—and more on what could be right: digging into the untapped business gains women's leadership can provide.

Ask yourself:

- What steps has my organization taken?
- With what results?
- How well equipped am I, really, to distinguish women's leadership?
- What specific steps have I taken to leverage the value of women's leadership?
- And why would I?
- Am I clear on the value?
- Do I know the business case?

The Transition to Value Model

Our opportunity now is to recognize that women's leadership is essential for remarkable corporate performance. Let's start with the most plain and simple fact: it's not a problem; it's an opportunity. We can start by shifting our thinking, using the Transition to Value Model.

From	To
Social justice	Value
Special	Essential
Silence	Speech

This simple model helps us visualize what our workplaces might be like if feminine leadership was valued, seen as essential, and spoken about. Then it wouldn't be considered just the way that women lead or just the way that men lead; the full spectrum of leadership would be open to everyone to choose how to express their own leadership traits and qualities.

The data is very clear about the value proposition of gender-balanced leadership. As we saw in chapter 1, the value is irrefutable. The transition we now need to make is to live in that story, and we need common language around it. We need distinctions that allow us to see what it is women are doing, when they do it, and the value added to our organizations, teams, and companies.

Up to now, initiatives to improve gender balance have focused on basic matters of what I call *corporate hygiene*:

- Equal pay
- Accommodations for work-life balance
- Women's leadership networks
- High-potential women's leadership programs
- Women's leadership employee resource groups (ERGs)

In these situations, any effort to establish gender balance is focused on compliance and addressing a problem. These types of initiatives are usually funded from a cost center and are separate from the "real business." It comes as no surprise that they are not taken seriously.

These initiatives and projects are usually set up with the good intention of supporting women. But they are also there to make sure that the company is keeping up with appearances. No matter what the numbers say, the company looks like it is making a solid effort to improve its gender balance. This is particularly true in countries where there is no gender-balance legislation, and these efforts are made to appease shareholders and stock markets. So far, the outcome is that we have spent more than 100 billion dollars and have produced less than a 1% per year change in gender balance.

We need to focus on when the real value happens:

- New leadership capabilities are recognized.
- A gender-balanced community with common language and purposes is established.
- 100% Capacity Leadership is operationalized.
- We can report on the measurable performance impact on the Big 7 corporate performance metrics.

When companies focus on 100% Capacity Leadership, gender-balance initiatives are centered on value and contribution. They are part of normal business, applied to real-world problems and opportunities, and are measured using regular business metrics. In other words, everyone is measured on the full spectrum of leadership traits and qualities, and we see measurable, positive impact on the Big 7 corporate performance metrics.

Putting It Into Speech and Action

This is your invitation to learn how to play a radically different leadership game. This new game generates a significantly better payoff on *all* measures—not only the indicators we've been trained to notice but also the ones that we understand on a gut level really matter for both professional and personal success.

Language enables us to share our thoughts, but it can restrict our thinking if we have not developed the words for concepts or things we have not previously experienced. Words can also restrict us if we become so wedded to a specific traditional or broader cultural definition that we are unaware of other possible interpretations. These new interpretations may present alternative, expanded options.

Most of the work on women's leadership comes from the masculine perspective, and it has taken the form of pushing and **focused action**. The feminine perspective has often been marginalized in business. The model I am sharing with you begins by mapping what we *value* as masculine and feminine, and looking at how what we *value* drives our desires and determines what we create. This language will enable women to share with other women, as well as for men to understand, so that together we can shift the leadership game to a more effective and more profitable level.

To look at it another way, every specialized body of knowledge has its own vocabulary, which is required because those specialists need to talk about the nuances and details essential to their field. Those specialists have words for things outside the common vocabulary, because they are making distinctions that are valuable to them and to what they do.

Business leadership language has historically revolved around the traditional masculine model. Given that up to now we haven't recognized that men and women lead differently, we have yet to develop language around the distinctions between the masculine and feminine styles of leadership, aka 100% Capacity Leadership. With this understanding, we don't end up pigeonholing ourselves in one or the other. Instead, we can transcend the binary and explore and engage as we seek what is most effective for ourselves, our customers, and our colleagues. When something doesn't have a name, you don't notice it's there. Or, as in the old proverb about the men trying to describe an elephant, you only see the parts instead of the whole. This nearsightedness can lead to the misunderstanding that the separate parts are all there is—thereby missing out on something bigger or on the value of the parts as a whole. Because we have lacked language for feminine leadership—which incorporates listening, inclusiveness, using different perspectives, and recognizing and legitimizing the value and power of individuals—we've not seen or fully grasped it.

In this book, we are using a new language of leadership. To get there, we're exploring new distinctions about the way men and women lead that gives us a new way of seeing and speaking about leadership to get us to an entirely different way of leading that we previously didn't have proper words to discuss.

For example, masculine values include **action**, **logic**, **competition**, and **quantification**; since we recognize these as distinctions and have language to validate them, we see these values and design our systems around them. But the feminine values of **appreciation**, **gratitude**, **attribution**, and

validating have not been recognized as valid or useful tools, because the distinctions around those values haven't been developed. When those leadership tools were used at all, it was piecemeal for whatever momentary problem needed a quick fix, but those tools are not seen as part of an interwoven value system.

Using one value system without the other leads to an imbalance. Once you understand the distinctions and can see the masculine and feminine value systems, it's possible to combine them into a more balanced approach. Integrating both value systems recognizes the complementary strengths and synergy inherent in the two systems, creating better overall results.

Why haven't we created distinctions and language around these concepts before now? Unhealthy or unbalanced actions lead to more of the same in response. This kind of action is cyclic; it can only repeat itself. We are all responsible for how we got to this place. But now that we realize that we have been out of balance and missing valuable tools, we can heal what's unhealthy and do better. Understanding is the first step to taking responsibility, which will enable us to find better solutions.

This is our opportunity to better understand what problems women's leadership can resolve, what value this style of leadership brings, why it is unique, and why that value can in turn add value for those around us and for those in our community. Likewise, we have the opportunity to decrease the cultural stigma attached to this style of leadership, which allows for all people to use these skills to lead in a different yet legitimate (and very effective) way.

Here's a key takeaway: if you operate within hierarchies exclusively, you lose out on ideas, input, and possibilities. The resulting culture leads to disenfranchisement. When you merge the tactical benefits of one style with the increased value and communication benefits of the other style, you create a culture in which all participants are valued, heard, and able to contribute from a place of respect and personal power, which yields more input, better ideas, and more sustainable, robust long-term success.

We've All Been Bob

So how do we talk the talk and walk the walk? How do we stop being like Bob and assuming that masculine traits and leadership are the same thing?

On an international consulting project, my team and I worked with a large transport provider. In this traditionally male-dominated industry, a new upstart company had begun to win over some of their most valuable customers. They couldn't understand what the appeal was; in conversations about their (very recently developed) competitive strategy, it was really apparent that, up to this point as the incumbent gorilla in their market, they had never needed to do any more than what they were already doing in order to succeed.

Sitting around their executive boardroom, they used language like "This is a war" (**aggression**); "We will just buy the damn business if we have to" (**arrogance**); and "They have no idea that they brought a pea shooter to a gun fight" (**domination**). While this seemed quite anachronistic, it probably reflected the reality of their world before they had lost 15% of their market share, including their top twenty customers, and two of their top producing salespeople—both of whom, as it happens, were women.

Over the course of a six-month project, we worked with the leadership team to break down what worked and what didn't. Of the fourteen-person executive team, ten came to us individually and confided that they really wanted to change. They saw the toxic groupthink at play across the enterprise but didn't know how to fix it. There was a lot of history and identity wrapped up in how this company conducted business; the CEO's last name was the name over the door, and he was the third generation of his family to run the company. There wasn't a lot to suggest that this was going to be an easy project, but it ended up being a really rewarding one.

As every quarter progressed, it became more apparent that change was necessary. The CFO was one of the greatest advocates for a new approach, and working closely with him, we modeled scenarios that allowed the leadership team to see what the future might look like, based on the choices they made along the way. A critical component of this was walking them through the 100% Capacity Leadership Compass, which we're about to discover in chapter 3. This was a turning point, as it let them identify the behaviors that were inhibiting their ability to compete and gave them a highly relatable model to guide their new behaviors. With a strong business case and hard data, together we could identify what behaviors had brought them to this situation (predominantly the unhealthy masculine)—and now they had a compass that could guide their future actions.

We were able to appeal to their healthy masculine traits like **security, providing, protecting,** and **competing** (against a standard of excellence, not 1:1). They honored those values with real live data from the scenarios and then called out the unhealthy masculine characteristics that they recognized they needed to move away from (**aggression, blaming, arrogance, hyper-acting**). By providing them with a highly actionable alternative that included healthy feminine characteristics—such as **respect** for their competition, **perceiving** what questions they really needed to ask, developing the resilience to go back to lost customers, and receiving their help to understand what went wrong—the executive team developed a whole set of practices that organically spread deeper and deeper into their organization. One executive even had a listening lunch with one of the women reps who left. He learned a lot and, with this new gender-balance lens, could actually hear what she communicated.

Over the following three quarters, the company won back a few of their old customers and within a year had also rehired one of the defecting sales reps.

This was a great project and an endlessly repeatable one. As humans, we have the gift of both the feminine and the masculine; it's an aspect of humanity that we really don't have the power to change, but we can understand and leverage it. We can cultivate gender balance within ourselves, our teams, and our companies and gain both personal and corporate performance benefits. By breaking out of the somewhat childish stereotypes that are often ascribed to gender and seeing the value that these balanced characteristics can bring to us, we can *be more.*

3

Seeing It in Action

Meet Evelyn

Evelyn is the global head of payment products for a thirty-billion-dollar financial services company. She has 180 product leads, innovators, and implementors reporting to her. Evelyn has been in this role for two and a half years. She loves what she does—it's amazing to see the impact new products have on customers' lives, as well as the bottom line, and the feedback and recognition she's received in both of those areas drives her to succeed. It can be a challenge sometimes to identify why other parts of the organization haven't been able to achieve the same level of success as her teams. She repeatedly tells people there are no secrets: it's all about understanding what the customer really values and what they want to make happen. This is an example of the feminine leadership approach of strategic **relating**.

This is the same for the B2B product group she runs now—in fact, it's even more critical. When she delivers this message, though, it seems to fall on deaf ears, and the conversation invariably turns to technology, technology, and more technology. She's an engineer; it's not like she doesn't get and love tech—she's probably more current than most of the other VPs. She's even been invited to speak at major vendor events, but "tech for the sake of tech," while convincing yourself that you are serving your customers, does nothing for her. She's even been told that she is "not technical" by people less qualified than she is (**bullying**). She stopped listening to that one a long time ago.

She knows she leads differently than her male counterparts, and lots of her team members have told her that (**appreciation, inclusion**). She's tried to "put a finger on it," but a big part of it is, quite frankly, being a woman leader. She doesn't need to win in every conversation (**accepting**); she has her eyes on bigger fish, like market share, customer share of wallet, and how much revenue they consistently drive from new product innovation (**context**). Her problem is: How do you tell a team of male leaders that to be successful, they need to behave like women?

It's beginning to be a bit of a pressing issue for her. Some of the amazing women she's hired, invested time in, and developed over the last few years aren't thriving, and one of her absolute stars resigned last month to start up her own e-commerce company. She's still in touch with her, and they're great friends; when she asked her why she left, she said she was sick of beating her head against a "bro wall."

An astonishing 45% of senior women executives leave large corporations to start up their own businesses. This is pretty incredible, because if work-life balance is supposed to be critical, how is it better in a start-up? What's becoming apparent is corporate life in many of its forms is innately unappealing to women, and even women like Evelyn, who've made it work for them, have a hard time explaining exactly *why*.

Evelyn knows she's great at what she does, and she's justifiably proud of her achievements. Her **resilience** has really served her, and she's earned the **respect** of her colleagues, which has given her the **flexibility** she needs to maintain a **stillness** in how she works, and to **observe synchronicity**, something she loves doing and considers to be her "superpower."

The challenge she has is really common, despite current efforts to develop and retain female executives. According to a survey conducted by the Society for Human Resource Management, nearly half of all workers (47%) cited work-life balance as the most important factor in their job satisfaction, and more than one-third (35%) said they had left a job in the past because it did not offer the work-life balance they were seeking. Additionally, a report by the Center for American Progress found that women are more likely than men to report that their work schedule conflicts with their personal or family responsibilities. Basic math tells us that this problem isn't going anywhere fast. Even seemingly critical issues that have been legislated for in many high-income countries, such as gender pay equity, aren't having the impact they absolutely must have if we're to move beyond "best efforts."

Building on the two previous chapters, let's help Evelyn identify what she does that enables her success and the success of the people around her. We're going to give Evelyn the language to discuss this beyond the context of gender and, in doing so, give her the power to pursue greater levels of corporate performance that gender balance enables: the Big 7, which I introduced in chapter 1.

How Women Lead

Because we don't have any real language for understanding what it is women are doing as part of their leadership, we don't see what makes women's leadership different from men's—and we don't understand and appreciate the diversity among women leaders either. We want to use the best of men's and women's leadership styles and to transcend the simplistic binary—so both women and men can express both our masculine and feminine leadership. But to be able to transcend the binary, we first need to understand it. If both men and women were asked to describe the woman whom they most admire and respect as a leader, they might not necessarily see the continuity across many women.

Let's take an example of an executive who is considered by her employees to be a strong and healthy leader. She is seen as a positive growth enabler for those around her. One of her core skills is listening, which, based on my research, is a core feminine leadership competency. How does she use listening at work? How valuable is that for her? Maybe it's important for her to hear different opinions and ideas before settling on a matter. She is unlikely to go into a meeting and say, "Do it like this." She is more likely to attend a meeting and listen to what people think the different issues are, to see the alignment and misalignments across the team. She can compile all that information, synthesize, and then say, "Well, I think that this is the right path to take based on everything that everyone just shared with me." Likely she will take feedback, and perhaps she's wrong. However, she is using those listening skills to at least generate ideas as to how to solve a specific problem.

Another capability that I've identified as part of feminine leadership is dialectic thinking—the ability to look at things from many different points of view and do high-level synthesis. This skill can create a sense of inclusion and ownership over the ideas and strategies deployed within companies. Think about someone with functional workplace empathy: she tries to put herself in the shoes of a client and consider the issues they have. What are they worried about? How can she sit back and use listening skills and negotiating skills with give-and-take, without predetermining the outcome? If there can be a common neutral ground, she can move forward and have a successful relationship from a long-term perspective.

My research points to this: men are more predisposed to **action**, and women are more predisposed to **perception** and **interconnection**. From a problem-solving standpoint, the ability to hold space for something unresolved is critical for evolved leadership. This is also where so much innovation springs from: the ability to sit with something and not have the answer right away allows us to think on a higher level about immediate issues. Likewise, linear, logical, deductive reasoning is what we have been taught in school; inductive leaps don't get you an A on your final exam. But women do often think more in inductive leaps, and we are now beginning to understand the importance of doing huge amounts of synthesis by being still, listening, and sitting with the problem, and then making an inductive leap. A balanced leader knows *when* to use both or either. A balanced leader also knows *how* to use both or either. For example, a good leader might do the interconnection and the listening, make sense of what they've perceived, and then focus in on what action needs to happen. A balanced leader might also circle back to the **perception** part of this process, or revisit the listening, in order to realign the **focused action**. The more skillful the leader, the more they are in the center of who they are as a human being, regardless of gender, and the more that they are using traits and qualities across this entire spectrum.

Let me give you three examples of rich veins in the gold mine of gender balance.

1. New Perspectives

We understand that if you want to do new things, you need to see new things and in new ways. This also means seeing actions, spaces, and relations between things in new ways. A more well-rounded approach balances patient inaction, wanting to do things together, being on a team, and getting stuff accomplished. Our ability to recognize **interconnection** allows different thinking to come in: asking how people, projects, and plans will be affected; what will happen beyond what we can immediately see; and what we are not paying attention to. Those are long-term questions that require a deeper level of presence. Women leaders tend, in general, to be more effective at that. The strong **focus** characteristic of masculine leadership is hugely powerful and relevant for getting things done, but it also tends to produce a narrowness that can lead to missing important things. A balance leads to bigger, better, more rounded results.

2. Decision-Making

A well-balanced team is better equipped to make decisions. This does not, of course, play out only along gender lines. Different people have different decision processes; we all have our own internal balance and our own ways of seeing and doing things. We need each of these approaches for innovation, customer engagement, and customer satisfaction. Likewise, we need a balance of masculine and feminine approaches to decision-making. Logical decision-making alone is not balanced. Context-based decision-making alone can stall or slow down a process in its effort to gather all the right information. Inductive reasoning, by its very nature, needs deductive reasoning to create both creative tension and balance.

In business, there is an enormous focus on what needs to be done immediately. This immediacy does not allow us time to question the overall value for humanity or to ask what the larger impact of our actions might be. The reverse is equally true; taking absolutely everything into consideration can prevent us from moving at all and can lead us towards a sense of overwhelm in the face of all the possible considerations. It's like trying to boil the ocean.

We tend to imagine taking action as a solitary activity. It's a Western conception of **action**: a solitary, masculine practice. Maybe we imagine pushing a boulder up a steep hill alone; maybe we imagine a champion or an explorer. What we do not always picture is the explorer with her team, the warrior with his cadre, the mentor who trained the strong man or the world-class physician. We overlook the meetings that happen before a big decision is made, the quorum and the alliances. Convening is the necessary plasma from which effective solitary and collective action emerge.

3. The Art and Science of Convening

There is a stark contrast in experience and value between a gathering that has been thoughtfully and carefully convened and one that has not. Yet convening expertise is inadequately named and appreciated. Designing experiences in a holistic way includes attending to the journey between events, deliverables, or activities, so as not to overlook the white space as an area of opportunity and innovative potential. For me, this brings to mind our tendency to focus on programs, policies, process, and technology when we want to make change happen. We're more inclined to invest resources and attention in designing these things than we are to designing the space *in between* these things. When that happens, our leadership teams obsess over the engagement score rather than explore what the day-to-day experiences of our individual employees can tell us. We spend ages getting our respectful workplace policy right but skimp on coaching managers about the everyday practices that actually create a respectful, psychologically safe environment.

Our organizations strenuously exert themselves hiring the most sought-after top talent in the market, and then invest little or nothing in deliberately fostering effective collaboration between them, their teams, and their peers. We're all about the latest recruitment technology to support our "candidate experience" but are so busy that we use that fancy system to send bulk disposition emails to the candidates we meet with. We build an onboarding program and then have zero touch points with the employees unless they raise (or become) a problem. When team conflict arises, we call it "interpersonal" and point to the individual actors' personalities. This often leads to us overlooking the connections between them as sources of conflict: information flow, shared role clarity, understanding of team goals, and trust in leadership.

These examples feel a bit clumsy and obvious, but I'm sharing them because I think they're so common. Great convening takes into account the space between. Great conveners understand this, design for this, and leverage this, resulting in "magical" experiences that can transform a program, project, innovation, or strategy. We have all seen what can happen when we bring together the right people for the right purpose. This is how so many of us have received new opportunities, found the right employee, drummed up a new client, or struck an unexpected but valuable deal. The magic arises when the right people at the right level come together in the right room.

What if part of leadership was amplifying and engaging others by understanding how their traits and qualities complement each other? From there, we could produce incredibly powerful teams of leaders. If you want gender diversity to add value to your company, don't focus on counting heads. Focus instead on the business opportunity that can be solved with gender diversity, and define how women leaders need to open up the playing field to 100% of our capacity. This changes the way that we measure our total leadership capacity.

Nature Operates on a Spectrum

The world of work has begun to develop its understanding of gender in general, and there is enough research to support the reality of these differences. As we better acknowledge these differences, the questions become: How and what are women doing differently? When women lead, what exactly is different?

Organizations measure leadership using tools and tactics that align with typically masculine styles of leadership. When organizations search out leadership qualities, the lens of observation tracks qualities more easily observed among men.

This style of measurement has historical precedent. It comes from our long history of regarding qualities that define leadership as closely aligned, if not synonymous, with the masculine. In the process, we become collectively less equipped, trained, and positioned to witness how it is that women lead differently. I would estimate that one- to two-thirds—varying, of course, by individual—of what women do in leadership is different. In my experience, even one-third is enough difference to constitute new and diverse insight, valuable and unexpected outcomes, and novel perspective.

Inevitably there is a degree of overlap in style. Some of the typically observed leadership qualities run parallel; good leaders do embody a certain set of relatively unchanging traits, across genders.

I am interested in sketching the perimeter of how women lead, pointing out how we can better observe these different tendencies, and then looking at how these differing but adjacent traits and qualities can amplify and expand our understanding of leadership and our capacity to lead more effectively.

Imagine a team of people making a decision. If the team is all men leading with predominantly masculine leadership traits, they will tend to focus on **logic, deductive reasoning,** and a need for **action.** They may make hasty decisions without considering key influencing factors or possible outcomes. The demise of Lehman Brothers is a good example of this, or the fall of Enron.

If the team has a mix of genders and **logic, deductive reasoning,** and **action** are balanced with **context, inductive reasoning,** and **convening,** there would be a greater chance of asking, "For the sake of what? What is the purpose of this decision? Are there interconnected factors that we need to take into account? Will our decision have a domino effect? And if so, what type of effect? Are there other parties who will be impacted by our decision, and should we bring them together to understand their concerns?" Some decisions may take longer, but we may come to value that as a good thing because it creates less churn. More people may be involved in the process, but there will be more buy-in and less resistance. I am not for one minute saying that one is better than the other. I am saying that interweaving and respectfully valuing each approach will result in greater value for all concerned. It is not either/or, it's both/and, where the sum of the whole is truly greater than the parts.

The Compass for Navigating 100% Capacity Leadership

Knowing that gender-balanced teams achieve better business outcomes, the question is: How does that work exactly?

There is a healthy body of workbooks and research studies describing how men and women lead differently. These differences have been documented in case studies and examples, as well as in the necessarily narrow data sets of controlled research studies. These examples and data sets illustrate how gender-balanced leadership has worked for specific people in specific contexts and, by extension, what might be true for others.

Research data, case studies, and descriptions are critical for understanding. But if we want to "reverse engineer" why gender balance achieves such positive results so that we can apply it intentionally and get the most value from it, we need a working model of 100% gender-balanced leadership.

To develop this, I've established two unique lines of questioning that I believe lie at the heart of distinctions between masculine and feminine leadership.

1. How We Approach Our Work

Men and women tend to approach work along a continuum that looks like the figure below.

Perception, sitting quietly and making sense, is associated with feminine leadership styles. **Action**, jumping in and doing, is associated with masculine leadership styles. **Perception** and **action** are polar opposites. They are equally valuable and equally important. They cannot be done simultaneously.

How We Approach Our Work

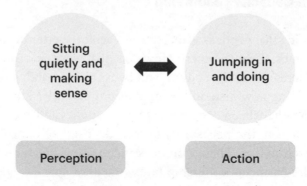

2. Where We Choose to Apply
Our Energy and Attention

Men and women tend to apply their energy and attention along a continuum that looks like the figure below.

Interconnection, putting energy and attention on the connections and spaces between things, is associated with feminine leadership styles. **Focus**, putting energy and attention on one thing, is associated with masculine leadership styles.

Where We Choose to Apply Our Energy and Attention

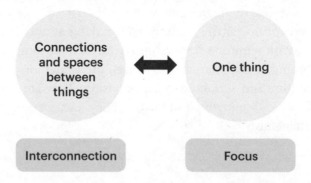

Focus and interconnection are polar opposites. They are equally valuable and equally important. They cannot be done simultaneously.

As with all binaries, there is, of course, a spectrum in between. But to transcend the binaries and open a space of greater understanding and more powerful innovation, we need to first understand them. This is the starting point.

Drawing the 100% Capacity Leadership Compass

Laying these four distinctions onto a compass creates the foundation of the 100% Capacity Leadership framework.

Exploring how the compass elements can polarize and amplify each other, and how each area is or isn't suited to specific business challenges, is a rich study that pays high dividends. Digging into these distinctions and helping clients apply them to achieve measurable gains is my primary work. So much is possible with 100% Capacity Leadership.

As a taste, here is a look at the distinctions in the hopes that they spark ideas about your business and your experiences.

The 100% Capacity Leadership Compass

Perception

Interconnection ← Focus

Action

The Halves

The compass can be divided in half. The lower right half is most related to masculine leadership, and the upper left half is most related to feminine leadership.

This simple binary is just the starting point. Digging deeper into the framework yields more valuable insights.

The Masculine Half

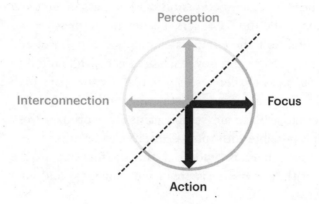

The Feminine Half

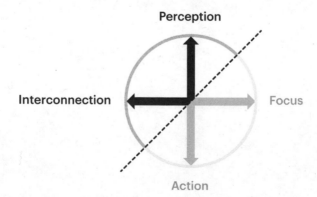

Compass Combinations

Exploring and naming the various compass combinations unearths valuable, observable, and repeatable patterns and practices that are applicable to specific business challenges. Working our way around the compass, we start with Focused Action, probably the most familiar leadership archetype and one of the most rewarded in business.

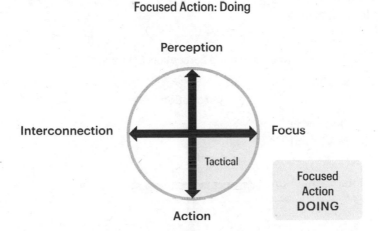

Focused Action: Doing

Focused Action: Doing

Doing, or focused action, is most typically associated with men.

Leaders who favor Doing are action oriented and fast moving, and they rely on the chain of command. Combined with other leadership styles, the leader who favors doing (The Doer) is a powerful results-getter who drives for strong outcomes.

When unbalanced by other leadership styles, those who favor Doing can push so hard to accomplish objectives—

to *win*—that little thought is given to the value of those objectives in a broader context. The Doer takes responsibility for results that are within their control and can be a micro-manager. In the extreme, overreliance on Doing can squash innovation by overvaluing deductive logic and demanding quick action. Hands up if you've ever been evaluated based on being "action oriented."

When unappreciated, leaders who rely mostly on Doing can become controlling and polarizing, vacillating between authoritarian drive towards goals and loyalty to team regardless of results.

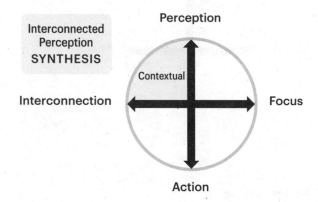

Interconnected Perception: Synthesis

Interconnected Perception: Synthesis

Synthesis as a leadership style is most typically associated with women.

Leaders strong on Synthesis traits are more aware of the interconnected nature of all things, and they foresee the potential results of actions—particularly as they relate to people, ideas, cadence, concepts, and structures. Combined with other leadership styles, the leader who favors Synthesis (The

Synthesizer) is a powerful, creative ally who combines systems understanding with inductive logic to identify low-friction, high-impact moves.

When unbalanced by other leadership styles, leaders who rely on Synthesis can get so wrapped up in possibilities that little is accomplished other than aspiring to boil the ocean. In the extreme, overreliance on Synthesis can cause manipulative, perfectionist behaviors in leaders who are unable to ask for help and have difficulty taking responsibility for failures.

When unappreciated, leaders who favor Synthesis can become agitated and polarizing, vacillating between righteous indignation and over-apologizing.

Focused Perception: Strategy

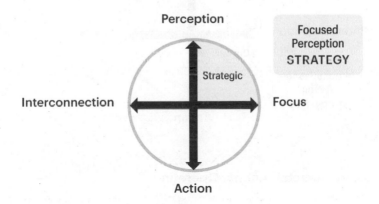

Focused Perception: Strategy

Strategy blends the more feminine trait of perception—understanding context—with the more masculine trait of focus.

Combined with other leadership styles, the leader who favors Strategy (The Strategist) is creative and is easily able to develop practical action plans that resonate in a larger context. Their ability to listen deeply within and beyond their

organizations brings them insights into the inner work-
ings of their business and generates strategies that are both
broad-reaching and realistic.

When unbalanced by other leadership styles, The Strategist may develop elegant, practical plans but have difficulty
putting their plans into operation. When fully valued, Strategy-
oriented leaders have an amplifying effect on all of the other
types of leadership.

Interconnected Action: Operating

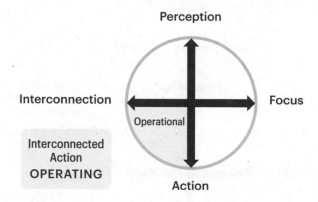

Interconnected Action: Operating

Operating blends the more masculine preference for **action**
with the more feminine preference for **interconnection**.

Combined with other leadership styles, the leader who
favors Operating (The Operator) brings both a desire and
capability for operational excellence to their organizations.
Balancing their bias for action with a deep understanding of
how things are interconnected means that they easily take
effective actions and empower their teams to do the same.

When unbalanced by other leadership styles, The Operator may become wrapped up in optimizing execution at the expense of recalibrating goals to adapt to changing circumstances. When fully valued, leaders who favor Operating have an amplifying effect on all of the other types of leadership.

The Full Compass

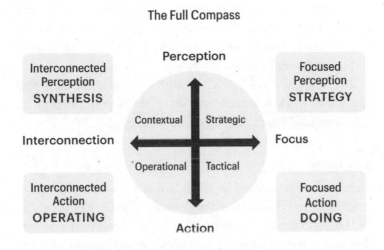

Using the Compass

Any person can learn to use any of the combinations in this compass, though some will come more naturally than others.

In business, the compass styles most associated with the feminine are not yet as well understood or used as the styles most associated with masculine leadership. In fact, some of the styles associated with women are mistakenly viewed as soft as opposed to essential.

The type of work that we have been trained to observe and value as strong leadership is most closely associated with masculine style—the focus is on a *thing* and the approach is *action*, which can be seen. Expressions such as "Throw some elbows!" "Break some china!" "Make it happen!" and "Get in there!" are standard in business. These all relate to observable work.

The work most associated with feminine leadership styles is not quite so visible. Sitting quietly and making sense does not look like anything is happening. The interconnections, or spaces between things and people, are also invisible. This can make women's leadership difficult to spot and understand. We will cover specific practices to help spot women's leadership in chapters 4, 5, and 6.

Let me give you a few examples of how the compass applies to work-related scenarios. I think you'll recognize how they could apply to you or a colleague.

Synthesis

Marie serves as director on the board of a government agency that oversees billions in redevelopment funds. Upon joining the board as a member of its audit committee, Marie senses that the agency's showcase project—construction of three new major public buildings—might be headed for trouble. Not wanting to jump to conclusions, she begins discreetly asking what she calls "strange questions" of the contractor and project oversight team—inquiries a little out of the ordinary. She then creates systemic guardrails by quietly adding three new items into the organization's existing risk and controls matrix. When implemented, the new controls are effective at repeatedly identifying and mitigating what could have become significant schedule delays and cost overruns. Three buildings have now been completed on time and under budget.

To the untrained eye, it might appear that nothing much happened. A new director joined the audit committee and asked to update the risk and controls matrix. Three building projects came off as planned. The relationship between these two events is not obvious, but it was fundamental.

Doing and Operating

Mark serves as VP of operations at an equipment manufacturer. His group has been stuck manufacturing a family of very old products with part counts in the thousands and production volumes as low as one or two units per quarter. Tasked from above with cost-reducing these old products by at least 10% within one year, Mark issues orders to his staff to force each supplier to lower its pricing by at least 10%. If they fail in this, their own and some of their teams' jobs are on the line.

His staff, along with their own direct reports, hold an emergency meeting to figure out what to do. The discussion is animated, but no one believes it is possible to negotiate cost reductions for thousands of items with minuscule purchase quantities. The volumes are also too low to cover the cost of offshoring production or to interest a contract manufacturer.

Rosie, a production planner on the team, sits quietly during the meeting, thinking. After the meeting, she talks to individuals across departments about a possible plan. This plan takes into consideration the supply chain as a whole and uses its biggest problem—low volumes—as the foundation for a solution. Over the next few months, the team works with suppliers and with the group's IT department to consolidate purchases and streamline receiving. This simplification results in some supplier cost reductions and reduces the number of staff needed to manage the supply chain. It also leads to fewer part shortages and lower overtime on the factory floor. Within less than a year, more than 10% savings is achieved—but not in the single-point-of-focus way Mark had originally mandated. In this instance, Rosie's work is recognized and rewarded, and she receives a promotion.

Strategy

Joining the R&D group of a major automaker, Tori is apprised
of an ongoing problem with on-road safety incidents for the
company's autonomous vehicle division. Traditional problem-
solving methodologies have been applied, and as each problem arises, its root cause is diagnosed and fixed. This is
turning into Whac-A-Mole. In addition, diagnosing the problems involves assigning specific blame, and tension within
the organization is getting high.

Tori maps out the individuals and roles in the organization
that could have input or bearing on the quality gaps, even
if they are not obviously connected. She speaks with many
individuals and small groups in the organization based on
her map. In conversations with "ivory tower" scientists and
engineers who make key decisions very early on in product
development, it becomes apparent that some early design
decisions could make it easier or harder for engineers later in
the product development process to avoid quality gaps. This
had not been obvious to them before. It is a joint discovery
during conversations based on the materials and information
she brought to them.

Once the ivory tower team sees the data and understands
the connection, they add new considerations to their design
parameters, and on-road safety incidents drop once the
changes take effect.

In this case, Tori does not appear to have *done* much, and
because the necessary changes were made at the very source,
only minor adjustments were needed to achieve significant
positive impact. But without seeing and valuing what she did,
we miss the opportunities to leverage her subtle genius again
and to recognize others with similar competence.

Evelyn Makes Gains

Trying to solve a problem using the logic that caused the problem in the first place won't bring you good results. We know this. Evelyn knows this. A lot of the effort that's gone into solving gender inequality has been amazing, it's been very expensive... and it's largely failed to deliver. So let's look beyond quotas and regulations and mandates at the underlying common sense that got us to where we are now. And let's take a moment to acknowledge all the effort that's been made, while simultaneously recognizing that if we're going to realize the awe-inspiring opportunity that gender balance can deliver, we have to make significant changes to our structures and our common sense.

Working within a product portfolio management team in a telecommunications equipment manufacturer, we observed exactly the kind of problems Evelyn is experiencing. A wonderful and highly successful product VP has reached a crisis point. The new products that the company was introducing were failing at an alarming level, but her portfolio was consistently performing. Engineers, who were paid bonuses based on the success of their products, were actively canvassing to join her teams, and she was being accused of favoritism by her increasingly hostile colleagues. Her more self-aware peers were asking her what she was doing differently, but she found it exceptionally hard to explain.

Evelyn helped develop some of the language and ideas you find here, and it was due in no small part to her **strength** and **resilience** that we were able to codify her superpower and eventually share it across the enterprise. Relating this to the 100% Capacity Leadership Compass, we can see that Evelyn has deep capability in both Synthesis and Strategy. She has very strong **perception** capability that spans both **Interconnection** and **Focus**.

By redesigning their processes to deliver much greater customer engagement, establishing robust practices to enable many more people to **observe synchronicity**, and coaching leaders on how to push back and question behaviors like **power over, threatening,** and **blaming**, which had become endemic within the product complex, the company was able to launch one of its most successful product suites ever. This was a real turning point, and using the same approaches, they went from strength to strength. In this case, the result of 100% Capacity Leadership impacted four of the Big 7: better strategy successfully capturing new markets, improved customer experience and retention, improved decision-making, and increased employee engagement as measured by their net promoter score (NPS).

How we're describing this may seem complex, and yes, things like customer-centric process mapping and complex process redesign are involved, but some of the actions that drove rapid and very real benefits were deceptively simple. An example of what drove better observation of synchronicity was a program we called Birds of a Feather. Evelyn's teams knew that she placed great value on sharing knowledge and teaching others about new ideas, so they had that internalized as a practice. Working with a gender-balanced team of three of her lead engineers and six volunteer engineers from other teams, led by Evelyn's peers, we instigated a topic table roster at lunch, where anyone across the entire company could join in on a conversation hosted by a product lead, and this simple practice of **convening** people developed bonds of trust and partnership. It drove the shift from an ego-driven **power over** mentality to an **accepting** power with worldview, which was grounded in abundance thinking and community.

4

Engineering New Value

Meet Tim

Tim is the CFO of a large multinational corporation; all told, 1,400 people spread across four locations report to him. This includes all financial processing, risk and compliance, treasury management, and mergers and acquisitions. The CIO and all IT functions report to him, as well as HR.

Tim is first and foremost a pragmatist. If it works, do it, as long as it's legal, decent, and honest. He believes businesses can get far too complex when they lose sight of what really matters: knowing who all the stakeholders are and what they really want and making sure that they know when they're realistically going to get it. This is his third C-level position; he's developed quite a reputation for financial transformation and for his vision of how corporations have a responsibility to drive a more balanced and enduring future for the communities they operate in. He sees it as being all about balance, in everything. He's fascinated by some of the leading thinkers in management science, but he finds a lot of what gets sold to him by big consulting firms to be seriously lacking in innovation.

He's really loved his career so far—it's given him so many opportunities—but he's really concerned about the status quo of the corporate world. There's a massive chasm emerging between established company leaders and the emerging workforce, and he doesn't see anything on the horizon to bridge that gap in an authentic and sustainable way. There's too much green-washing and pink-washing; the company's efforts so far to address gender balance have been pretty ineffective when you look at the real numbers. Measuring stuff like employee engagement really doesn't serve anyone, and those kinds of metrics don't make change happen. He sees it as a missed opportunity to make the connection between excellent leadership and outstanding results—financial results, that is; the real, measurable, and impactful stuff that stakeholders care about. Things like ERGs push the responsibility back on to the employee, and that's an abdication of leadership. If his company can get this right, and *really* make balance happen, he sees a dazzling opportunity, but looking at the people tasked with it, he has his doubts.

Tim has three amazing women reporting to him. And in his career, he once reported to a woman CFO. He learned a lot, and she was very generous in helping him learn and grow. He found himself being more engaged, and he felt more innovative. At least under her, there were less harsh consequences for taking measured risks and going after bigger results. He knows, from his experience, that women lead differently, and he's tried to lead and manage them differently, but he has no real insight into what he is doing. He feels like he is making it up as he goes along, flying by the seat of his pants, so to speak. Being a numbers guy, this makes him really uncomfortable.

He once did an unconscious bias workshop. He really appreciated what they were trying to point to, and he became more aware of some of his own biases. But the blame-and-shame vibe was a nonstarter for him. In addition, there was no framework or structure that would allow him to deliver measurable results. It seemed like a Band-Aid that was actually rubbing salt on the wound.

Tim has heard all the data from the big consulting firms on gender balance; while it's enticing, it also seems a bit hyperbolic, and he's not sure how to even go about implementing it (**logic**). Nor is he sure how to determine the measurable impact it could have for his own organization or company (**providing**). He'd love to deliver some of these returns for his company (**accomplishment**), and he has a strong sense that he has to start by developing a better understanding of what his female reports do when they lead differently (**predictability**). He has asked them, but they can't see their own brilliance—like a fish in water, he surmises.

Better Together

Instead of creating an us versus them mentality, let's create what a wise friend of mine calls a *we environment*, which is more powerful if we are truly committed to solving our collective problems. Not only that, but let's step back and see the real underlying problem.

Women don't need to be "fixed" to make them valuable, and they don't need to be taught to act more like men. This is the old, outdated, resource-wasteful story. We do not think less of a fruit tree when it fails to produce maple syrup! (Yes, this book had a Canadian editor!)

Women have innate leadership abilities that are already valuable, no intervention needed. What does need to be remedied is the lens through which we see women's leadership. So does the language that we use to describe that leadership so that the value can be perceived, recognized, and applied to the benefit of everyone. In other words, we need a new story.

By fixing the lens through which we evaluate women's leadership, everyone at the table will ultimately be able to recognize and value the complementarity of logic and context, the combination approach of blending step-by-step with inductive leaps, and the identification and factoring in of collateral impacts.

Adjusting our lenses requires a break from conventional wisdom, a change from the traditional way things have always been. We have been trained to elevate a style of masculine leadership. Maybe we read *The Art of War* in school, or maybe we heard about the valor of wartime emperor Marcus Aurelius. We have been encouraged to emulate that approach to leadership, often personified by unhealthy male leaders, even when evidence shows it can be limiting at best and self-defeating at worst. We remain stuck in common sense, as we saw in chapter 1.

Unfortunately, that frame of reference is not openly discussed, and so it is taken for granted. It remains unobserved (because we think it's just how things are); we can be misled into thinking it is inevitable and unchangeable. However, this is a learned way of thinking and doing. What is learned—consciously or unconsciously—can be unlearned and retrained, especially when the rewards—for individuals, groups, and the planet—for doing so are extremely valuable.

The Six Lenses of Value

If you've ever had an eye exam, you've sat down behind a phoropter. It's the machine the doctor has you look through, as they adjust one lens and then another, asking, "Which is better—one... or two?" By showing you a sequence of lenses, the eye doctor helps you choose the best combination to create perfect vision.

I've created a framework inspired by the phoropter that I call the Six Lenses for Seeing the Value of How Women Lead. But instead of the ophthalmologist's choice of "One... or two?" that depends on your particular vision, these lenses go from the older, worse way to the newer, better way. When you switch the lens, you see everything better. I hope it will provide a way for us to clear our collective vision of what feminine leadership is and how to change our approach so that we can all get better outcomes.

The Six Lenses for Seeing the Value of How Women Lead

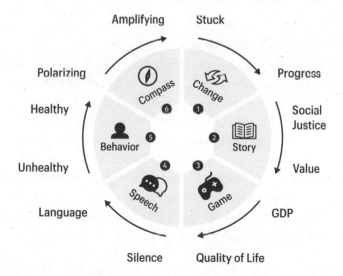

1. From Stuck to Progress

In the first lens, we begin by realizing that we need to do something to get women on board in a meaningful way. We are stuck, so we create change—things like more women earning degrees and pursuing careers outside the home. Women run for office and move into management positions. More women shift into very visible, high-profile positions. We achieve change—but there's still a fundamental divide that creates problems.

While women have the education and gain the experience, the glass ceiling is real and career-limiting. Women become frustrated, because they perceive that the system is rigged against them in both subtle and obvious ways. The initial story exposes the rigged game of sexism—that of unhealthy men building unhealthy systems that favor men who are just like them, and who are willing to reward unhealthy women— but only up to a point. Healthy women leaders—and healthy men leaders—who see that the flaws in the system are more complex than hiring percentages and graduation rates struggle to solve the problem.

2. From Social Justice to Value

In this second lens, the initial focus is on social justice and the unfairness of the system. And this is where we have been for the last fifty years, ever since Mary Tyler Moore tossed her hat into the air on that chilly Minneapolis morning. We hoped that bringing women into the workforce would change everything, and it didn't. Instead, it showed us that the problems were deeper rooted than we first thought, and that required analyzing a system that had been accepted as the way things are and developing language to explain what was really going on.

What has to happen in this second lens is to change the narrative. It was important to have the initial conversation about unfairness and social justice. But while social justice concepts are fundamental to our understanding of fairness and ethics, the narrative is also disempowering to both sides. It can trap both sides in negative roles, like insects in amber. And this lens is where we've stayed, because too often victims lack power to change the system, wrongdoers lack the will to change the status quo, and those who perceive themselves to be innocent bystanders or quiet allies feel unappreciated and unacknowledged. It's time to change the lens by identifying the value that women's leadership brings, and by developing the concepts, words, and messages to communicate how everyone benefits from that value. By focusing on the value that women leaders bring to the organization, everyone—all leaders, all team members, all stakeholders, and the world itself—wins.

3. From GDP to Quality of Life

Up to now, the game of business has been all about the GDP, or for an individual company, profitability. But the definition of profitability has been very narrow, focused only on income, money, and wealth. The modern concept of GDP was first developed by Simon Kuznets for a US Congress report in 1934. In this report, Kuznets warned against its use as a measure of welfare. This part of the memo we seem to have missed.

Since the focus has been so narrow, GDP and profit have been pursued without regard to the real costs   damage to the environment, physical and psychological unwellness due to stress, turnover, burnout, epidemic levels of job dissatisfaction, and the massive waste of human capital. While we are accustomed to hearing quarterly reports on stock market valuation, we have avoided balancing those gains against what it cost to achieve them. Yet the true costs are paid by everyone on the planet, in real dollars as well as in lives.

Absenteeism, mental health issues, and medical costs related to stress-induced illnesses cost society tens of millions of hard dollars a year, and millions more in lost productivity and personal income. Underemployment (the inability to find and sustain jobs that pay a living wage)—whether because of ageism, racism, sexism, homophobia, or other negative filters—inflicts huge societal costs, not to mention the impact on individuals and families and the next generation of citizens.

Environmental damage from climate change (contributed to, at least in part, by industrial waste and pollution) is on track to cost trillions of dollars in property damage, ruined fishing grounds, water scarcity, air pollution, rising sea levels, and harsher storms. A medical-pharmaceutical-insurance-industrial complex focused solely on profitability exploits the inflexible buying choices available to sick and dying people, while making it prohibitively expensive to maintain wellness, leading to an increasingly unhealthy population.

At this rate, we are in real danger of employment costing us a rich life.

But what happens if we change the lens to look at GDP and the Wellness Index, seeking a balance? Calculating gains by looking at the GDP alone is like determining a company's profits without subtracting expenses from revenue. Every corporate balance sheet shows both the money brought in and the money it cost to produce and distribute the product. If you can't cover your expenses, you don't make a profit, no matter how large your income appears to be. For too long, we have treated the GDP as pure revenue without balancing the books. When the goalposts of the game are money, power, and influence, then the GDP is the score by which the game is won. But it only measures half the game. Because by the goalposts of creation, balance, and interconnectedness, the Wellness Index is the other score that matters.

By recognizing the complementary, essential value that women's leadership brings to the game, we finally have a complete and much more accurate score to determine whether we are winning or losing. Now we can assess if we are in danger of "winning" ourselves into extinction by ignoring, underfunding, and underprioritizing actions and investments that address physical and psychological health and overall sustainability.

We have changed the game and made it something where the gains benefit everyone on the planet, instead of funneling the majority of the winnings to a small handful of people out of billions. And here's the best part—even that handful of people still win because of decreased costs to society and improved environmental sustainability.

John Gerzema and Michael D'Antonio did some fabulous work of exploring this relative value in their book *The Athena Doctrine: How Women (and the Men Who Think Like Them) Will Rule the Future*. They interviewed 64,000 people, from countries representing 65% of the global GDP. Of the people surveyed, 66% have felt influenced by the narrative that women think differently. People can see that difference in action—and not only do they like it, they prefer it.

4. From Silence to Language

Speech becomes the next important lens through which we view women's leadership. At first, there was silence, because no one felt a need to talk about something that they didn't notice and didn't think existed. Since then, we have struggled to wrap language around the differences—and their value—between how men and women lead. For most of that time, women who wanted rewards similar to those gained by men were told to act and react like men, to focus and evaluate like men, and to speak and prioritize like men.

That didn't work—but it did expose the fact that the game's rules and rewards had been twisted by unhealthy masculine leaders into something that most women and many men didn't want because it came at too high a cost.

One of the key reasons that telling women to behave in a masculine manner hasn't worked is because the masculine leadership models are largely based on the behavior of unhealthy masculine leaders. Women had the false choice of falling into the trap of behaving like unhealthy feminine leaders—the toxic complement to unhealthy masculine leaders' behavior— or replicating the behavior of the men themselves, which was unhealthy and unsustainable.

Traditionally, men's leadership has been rooted in quantification, competition, and accomplishment—attributes that can be measured, visualized, and demonstrated. But when we create language and distinctions about what women's leadership is, we see that it is rooted in creation, balance, and interconnectedness. These attributes are harder to measure and perhaps to visualize, which has slowed our development of the right words to use.

Look what happens when the two sets of leadership distinctions are made equal. We get **quantification/creation, competition/balance,** and **accomplishment/interconnectedness.** Done right, with both ways of leading equal, we have a path forward that tempers the self-destructive tendency to blindly pursue GDP and profit above all else.

When we identify, recognize, and assign worth to **listening, acknowledging, recognizing, relating, facilitating,** and **contextualizing**—all of which are hallmarks of women's leadership—we have a new language with which to talk about the value women bring to the table. If ego is driving competition, it can lead to a zero-sum game in which all players lose in the long run. But if equal voices urge balance and emphasize interconnectedness, the conversation is much more likely to seek out and pursue win-win scenarios. When accomplishment is only about checking off tasks, the negative long-term impacts caused by cutting corners, using problematic materials, engaging in unfair labor practices, or entering into questionable partnerships are more easily overlooked. Pair the drive to accomplish with an awareness of how every action causes an impact and a reaction with repercussions (a combination of context and interconnectedness), and many very expensive scandals and problems will be completely avoided.

5. From Unhealthy to Healthy

Behavior is the fifth lens, and we've looked at the healthy and unhealthy masculine and feminine behaviors throughout the book. When we understand that the healthy and the unhealthy aspects have to do with what has been recognized, rewarded, or adopted to survive in a toxic interpersonal relationship, we realize that these behaviors have nothing to do with men and women per se, and everything to do with the culture that teaches and rewards them.

Since unhealthy behaviors are not innate but learned, they can be unlearned, and healthy behaviors can be learned in their stead and rewarded in practice. This frees both women and men, dispenses with blame, and shifts the conversation towards moving forward together, using complementary values and skills, to create something better.

6. From Polarizing to Amplifying

That creates the sixth lens: moving from the polarization of blame, mistrust, and an us versus them mentality into amplification mode. What is amplification? It's the creation of an environment in which people's best traits and skills are seen. Ideally, we cultivate an environment where many sorts of leaders are understood, valued, and leveraged to achieve gains in both GDP and the Wellness Index.

You amplify only what you observe. Today, as I noted above, most companies only measure one type of leadership. This is a hangover from the '30s, '40s, and '50s, when the workforce was predominantly made up of men; as women entered the workforce, we didn't adjust our understanding of leadership; as a result, we are wasting about half of women's leadership capacity and damaging and undermining men's leadership capacity. If all that you measure is the masculine, men will tend towards more masculine leadership and abandon their more feminine leadership qualities, and the women will "lean in" and try to emulate masculine leadership—because that is what they get paid and promoted for—and in the process they, too, will abandon their feminine leadership traits and qualities. When we don't simply accept common sense, when we observe and understand, when we measure all aspects and talk about their value, we can amplify. Amplification is the result that becomes possible when we put what we've learned from the other five lenses to use to build a better workplace and a better future together.

The 100% Capacity Road Map: Six Key Steps for Mobilizing Change

Once we have seen with new lenses, how do we change what we do? These six steps are the essential building blocks of how we define, design, and deliver projects for organizations that want to increase their capacity for excellence.

1. Start with the End in Mind

Peter Drucker was right when he said that culture eats strategy for breakfast. I've always interpreted that to mean that shifting mindsets is the way to create truly transformational change, and truly transformational change will beat the best strategy any day.

This isn't an operational project: it's a transformational one. We're not going to be telling people what to do. We will be helping them to see a new possibility and define a solution to what they thought was an intractable problem. The process of cultivating new mindsets is the true north for this project, and to get it started on the right foot, we need to do something that some of us might think we don't have to the skills to do. But to succeed within any organization, we've already mastered some level of it. We have to *sell* our audience on the value of what we're going to do and clearly articulate what's in it for them.

2. Start Small

Start with a carefully identified, qualified, and contained project. This is the key to building momentum for any transformation. Over the years, I have discovered that this delicate process is best done small with a trusted team who are equal participants in the vision of the possible. We've been conditioned to see leadership as a somewhat solitary function, but this is the time to break away from that jaded interpretation and start building our own sense of power with, and not power over. This small nucleus will form the catalyst that discovers the real leadership capacity throughout your organization, and this first pilot project is their on-ramp to that journey.

3. Make Sure You Know Where You're Taking Them

I've never been a fan of the "project as journey" metaphor—
I find it slightly patronizing—but in this particular case, it is
a journey! As a result, you need to know where you are taking
people because you're both a scout and a guide, and while
some ambiguity is inevitable, it's very overwhelming to lack a
clear definition of success. I suggest scouring your work experience for material. Look for a project that you can transform.
As the scout and guide, it's important to pick a project that
is a stretch to achieve but still has a high chance of success.

You must pick a first project where the results will be measurable, noticeable, and valuable and the primary beneficiary
of the transformation will be an enthusiastic customer. I rec-
ommend that you pick one area from the Big 7 that has good
corporate metrics in place or, alternatively, one that at least
has an established baseline. For example, if you were to pick
innovation because your company has had difficulty getting
products to market, or is even living off a decent product
portfolio but nothing new is showing up on the horizon, you
can generate very significant metrics that leaders are probably already aware of—and perhaps even a little terrified by!
If it's an area the organization has struggled to transform for
the last two to three years, perhaps failing to bring new products to market successfully or experiencing a high turnover of
product leaders, starting your project with a goal of launching
a new product and achieving an ambitious level of growth
will attract a lot of positive attention.

4. Know Where You're Leaving From

This is a unique way to choose to achieve operational success,
and it's a powerful one. It's critical that before you start, you
establish a baseline from a gender-balance perspective. Use

the simplified 100% Capacity Maturity Model to establish your starting line. It will help you more confidently make the connection between the value you generate and the approach you've taken, which makes spreading the message of 100% Capacity Leadership a lot easier.

This simplified version of the 100% Capacity Maturity Model below allows you to score your company to determine your 100% Capacity Leadership maturity. There are five scoring columns. Enter a score for each row to see where your company stands and where there is room for improvement. The maximum for each row is 8, and the total for the model is 24. It gives you a good baseline.

100% Capacity Maturity Model

	Blissful Ignorance (0 Points)	Aware/ Considering (1 Point)	Implementing (2 Points)
Individual woman focused	Few, if any, women in company	Formal program in development (e.g., pay review)	Gender-diversity program has been formalized
Program focused	No initiative planned or underway	Aware of gender-diversity industry PR expectations	Women leadership and retention program in place
Transformation/ ROI focused	All critical components of gender-diversity infrastructure absent	Oblivious to ROI opportunity	Growing awareness of own ROI; preliminary research

Transforming (4 Points)	Amplifying (8 Points)	Score
Executive team educated on thinking, practices, leadership, and potential ROI of 100% Capacity Leadership	Focus on amplifying the capabilities of genders as strategic advantage	
100% Capacity Leadership program in place, with supporting policies, processes, and technology	Transparency around all policies; metrics integrated into strategy and standard operating procedure	
Multiple projects identified for 100% Capacity Leadership ROI	ROI published and 100% Capacity Leadership included	
		Total Score _____ /24

5. Personally Pick the Best Team for This Work

First and foremost, make sure your team manifests the balance that you're looking to drive. As we know, this isn't just about gender, and it's important to make that clear. You're emphatically *not* looking to solve an inclusion problem; you're using the power of gender-balanced leadership to solve an operational challenge that has resisted traditional approaches. Make sure you choose people who have the personal capacity to self-observe and the ambition to deliver, and avoid the pitfall of choosing your team based only on their current level of expertise.

The best candidates are:

- Reporting directly to directors or VPs
- Being groomed to step up and lead people or key strategic initiatives
- Current managers who can level up to take on more leadership
- Committed to growing their careers as innovation leaders
- Managers who are committed to growing others

This is a good moment to assess where you want to position yourself. Before taking on the project of transformational leadership and implementing these practices and concepts with a small team, consider your role and your ideal role at work. Are you an emerging leader?

- Leading a team or getting ready to lead a team
- Looking to level up the people around you
- Can be in any function
- Customer focused
- Outcome focused

- Responsible for a defined project associated with or fully encompassing an objective or key result (OKR)
- Keen to make offers above and beyond your current job description
- Reading, studying, or watching educational videos
- Have high potential to add ongoing, long-term value to your company
- Past performance must exhibit high-potential capability

6. Live and Breathe the Narrative

It starts with you: you are the ambassador for this new approach, and as such, you must be well versed in the why, the how, and the what. Later in the book, I'll give you specific examples of metrics you can draw from to build your business case, and you can add to these with your own successes over time. To begin with, though, make absolutely certain that you talk about compelling, measurable, and valuable operational outcomes every time you discuss your project, which makes the connection for people between the ambitious results you want to achieve and the different approach you're taking to deliver on them. Early in my career, I worked for a wonderful partner in a large international consulting firm who counseled all of his managers to "write the final report for every project on Day One." This seemed odd at the time, but once you've done it, it's a wonderful discipline. It helps you stay focused on that success. To make the success very personal, it's worth working out and practicing your own "case study" presentation early on in your project, and sharing it with your team, as it will give power to your transformation message and make your presentation more compelling.

Operation Tim

We started an initial project with Tim and a shared services organization that reported to him. This group was within a large and rapidly expanding commercial distribution company. The objective of the project was to solve an operational problem: their finance function was seen as a barrier to getting business done by pretty much everyone, except themselves. Staffed predominantly by women, they were seen as the "compliance cops," and this was having a severe operational impact in some areas. Because of this prevailing distrust, contracts that should have been verified before being sent to the client were rushed through order entry at the last minute, frequently booked at the quarter, and then a week or so later unbooked when inconsistencies were discovered. There was lots of finger-pointing. One of the reasons why Tim thought gender was an issue was an incident with a sales RVP, who had asked him if he could send out some of the men from the finance team, because "they understand the urgency in a way none of the girls seem to."

Tim knew that some of this was growing pains: the regulatory requirements they had to follow were a symptom of their amazing success, and every business leader in the company knew they were absolutely necessary. He didn't think that everyone on his team was an angel, but he could see that at the root of these problems was systemic distrust, and he was really uncomfortable with how gendered the problem had become.

We started a pilot project with the North American commercial teams. We put together a team of fifteen contracts people and fifteen salespeople. We worked with them to examine their prevailing common sense and to design how they could engage more effectively. The common sense of the contracts team was driven by a need to understand **context** and an appreciation of the collateral impact of the decisions about contract approval. The common sense of the sales team originated from a need for **action, competition**, and getting it done.

With an understanding of how each saw and approached the process and an appreciation for why, we set about designing shared standards to support the shared process. We did this over a few weeks, and as a team, we undertook four to five other subprojects over a period of nine months. The project was enormously successful and generated rapid results, such as a 22% reduction in order errors and a 10% reduction in order processing costs. Tim was an eager participant at every stage. He absolutely loved the idea of driving the organization to 100% Capacity Leadership and saw it as his biggest opportunity to "amplify."

Working with Tim, we developed a 100% Capacity Leadership template for each of the Big 7, as these are the areas where we typically see businesses drive the most impact. What has the organizational impact been like? Well, pretty significant across multiple areas, and the gender-balanced approach continues to drive market advantage, stronger recruiting performance of qualified diverse candidates, better retention, and improved customer satisfaction. Success at leading gender balance actually *is* business success.

5

What Works and
What Doesn't

Meet Vera

Vera is the head of document processing for commercial lending at SoBank, a top five national bank. Two hundred and fifty document processors report to Vera. Her department has a loan throughput of three billion dollars annually. Vera is kind of a big deal. She has made so many sacrifices to succeed at work that she literally feels nauseous when some perky HR person rocks up and talks about a "women's ERG." Where were these people when Vera found out she was paid a fraction of what her less successful, less qualified, and less competent male peers were paid? They told her there wasn't anything they could do about it, and it was because she'd "chosen the mommy track." She has ten years to go before her planned retirement, and she will be very financially secure, because she made sure that was the case, no thanks to anyone in HR or any ERG. She's phenomenal at what she does, she's delivered massively for this company, and she's really going to miss her work, but she can't afford to ever appear vulnerable, so it's head down, nod politely, and keep her eyes on the prize.

She has always worked well with her male peers. Over the years, she has learned to put up with their egos and attitudes. While she'd love to be able to form real partnerships with them, what she has works fine for now. And she has learned to not speak her mind and to go along to get along. She knows the company is missing out, but after years of trying, she simply does not seem to be able to help her male counterparts see what she sees. She pays attention to how people are connected. She sees who builds trust with whom and where. She sees how people respond under pressure and who can remain calm in a crisis (**relating**). She knows how people, processes, and systems work together. Through her own painful experience and deep perception, she has seen how changing one can dramatically impact the other, either well or disastrously. So, she can see the impact of different moves and decisions (**context**). When she feels she is in over her head and needs to call in an expert from her team or another department, she knows how to ask for help and park her ego (**accepting**).

She does what she can to implement her own thinking into her department's processes and to train the people around her to understand what she has done. She knows that when she leaves, many, if not all, of the customer listening processes she has implemented will be removed by someone who does not see what she sees. A few people on her team really get it, and she's so proud of them, but she feels a bit guilty about what will happen to them. She keeps telling them to "accept the things they can't change, change the things they can, and, most importantly, learn to tell the difference."

Javier, one of her best-performing managers, tells her that given how massively successful her department has been over the years, she actually has the power to change a whole lot more than she thinks she can. He even told her that he heard through the grapevine that the CEO personally ensured Vera's parking space was closest to the front door, because he didn't want her walking in the rain! This made her laugh, but yes, she got his point. The CEO took a personal interest in her success and made an effort to demonstrate he personally valued her contribution.

Everything was just fine as far as Vera was concerned, until the news of yet another acquisition hit the wires. It was a really interesting one, in an adjacent vertical and quite "innovative." The CEO asked her to take a look at the processes within the company before anyone else even knew about it. He knew that she would be thorough, completely trustworthy, and discreet. When she examined the processes in the company they were thinking of acquiring, she was shocked by how far behind and manual many of their processes were. It was retail lending on a massive scale, so while the deal values were much, much smaller, the volumes were huge. She was pretty excited about the improvements that could be made quickly and quite cheaply, and about the customer and employee experience improvements they could deliver. It was exactly the area her star manager Javier had mastered so well in her current team, and it was a challenge not to tell him about the opportunity—she knew he would be so excited!

When she delivered her assessment report to the CEO, she used exactly the same format that had been well received before: her assessment of their situation, the processes, customer focus, technology, and team, followed up by her immediate recommendations, and the value that those recommendations could generate. She found it amusing that the CEO used that exact format to present the information to all the other people on the evaluation team (he'd asked her permission beforehand). So far, so good! She was looking at some pretty great option grants at year end. If the CEO was appreciative, and if they got the integration right, her stock would multiply in value. Pretty incredible for a girl from the wrong side of nowhere!

The massive kicker though? The CEO pulled her aside before the acquisition announcement and told her he wanted her to run the integration project and deliver on the processing center she had recommended in her report. He couldn't have made a better offer: she'd be reporting directly to him, her salary would be increased significantly, she could handpick her team, it went on and on—but she totally wasn't ready for this! She was counting down the years to a nice early retirement, not planning on taking the helm of an exciting new challenge. She recommended that he give it to the EVP of Customer Experience in the new company. The CEO looked at her and said, "Do you mean the one you said 'had never actually met a customer in his five years in the role, showed no interest in his team's development, and focused exclusively on managing up'?"

She needed some time to think about this. He told her he could only give her twenty-four hours and that he was relying on her to make the right decision for herself, her team, and the company. She asked if she could talk to her team about it first; she couldn't do it without them. He smiled and said he thought she'd ask that and that the COO had provisionally blocked some time in their calendars, so Vera could schedule a team meeting, and he would be there to support her in the meeting and throughout the whole process.

She knew she could do it, that wasn't the issue; her challenge was how on earth could she engage with all of the department heads in this massive new company, as well as her own, and guide them through the change? The COO was a good guy: he knew his business and had been a real supporter in the past, so she was glad his role was secure, but he was *so* rigid in how he ran his own team and had a very transactional focus. Admittedly, there was really no way she'd work for the "new guy"—he was all about his connections and obsessing about what everyone thought of him. Politics, politics, and more politics; there was no way he'd have the resilience necessary for this big of a role.

While she knew every mother's goose is a swan, she really did believe that the biggest mess to clean up was in the new company: their costs were insane, everyone competed with each other constantly, the micromanagement of data was driving all of the wrong behaviors, employee turnover was off the charts, and the people who stayed felt victimized. With her existing management team, a few new promotions she'd been wanting to make anyway, and the few strong performers she'd met during the evaluation project, she absolutely knew she could make this work, and then some. Was she talking herself into it? She put on her favorite playlist and started to think.

How You Lead Expresses Who You Are

How we lead is an expression of who we are, in terms of how we see the world: how we interpret things, how we make sense of things, how we learn, how we evolve. This can be seen in the How You Lead Expresses Who You Are Model.

The How You Lead Expresses Who You Are Model

Generating		What do they CREATE in the world?
Practices		What are they recurrently DOING?
Desires		What do they WANT?
Being		How do they SHOW UP in the world?
Essence		What can you rely on them to BE?

Desire Is the Engine of the Universe

This model starts in the center, because the center is what drives us. What do you want? What matters to you? What difference do you want to make in the world? What difference do you want to make for your friends, family, yourself? What do you desire?

The phrase "Desire is the engine of the universe" has been attributed to many sources: the Talmud, the Koran, Einstein... who really knows its origin? We can decide to just accept it as a useful piece of wisdom. Desire drives how we lead and how we show up as leaders at work and as teammates, parents, friends, and contributors. It's what drives the expression of our leadership. Knowing this, we can see our own strongest impulses generate whatever natural practices we engage and what we might generate in the world. These manifest in the traits of healthy and unhealthy masculine and feminine leadership.

I introduced these distinctions in the introduction, and I've highlighted them as we've moved through the book. By now, like the Iso E Super molecule, you are probably beginning to recognize these traits and qualities in yourself and in your coworkers, and you are working to see, hear, and value them. You are figuring out how to amplify each other's fabulous traits and qualities. Look again at my list of healthy and unhealthy masculine and feminine leadership traits, and you will see how it all falls into place and how they express who you are in how you lead.

Being Is How You Show Up in the World

Being is how you consistently show up. How do other people see you or experience you in action or presence as they engage and work with you? Do they see you as **in action, providing, protecting, competing**? Or do they see you as **receiving, perceiving, accepting, relating**? Or some wonderful, valuable mixture of these traits? Do they speak of these traits in a naive shorthand as "kind," "ambitious," and "driven" without necessarily stopping to think of why? Where might these qualities come from? Why are you expressing them as you are? If I can understand what you want and how you go about getting it—how you show up—I can engage much more effectively with you, and we can begin to co-invent and maybe even innovate together.

Your Essence Is What We Can Always Rely On You to Be

This is your go-to place—your presence. The position from which you derive your capability to lead. As you can see from the healthy and unhealthy traits list, this covers traits like **patience, playfulness, action orientation, steadfastness,** strength, flexibility, stillness, resilience, and persistence. It's how others see the essence of you when you are at your best or worst!

Your Practices Are What You Recurrently Do

How does this all come together in what we do at work and in life? It's interesting to note that the masculine *doing* is more literally doing. It's making things, constructing, setting up procedures, oberving repeatable actions. Whereas the *doing* with feminine energy is gratitude, appreciation, stillness (enabling others to feel heard), and observing synchronicity. You can see that in a world where physical action is prized, the feminine type of doing can be misunderstood and the value can be missed.

Generating Value for Others
Is How You Create in the World

In the world, at work, and in our communities, we can create safety, security, material well-being, shelter, beauty, abundance, newness, and balance. These traits amplify each other, making our lives more enjoyable and richer. One without the others is a poorer experience. We have the opportunity to create balance, which enables us to generate more value for ourselves and others.

We have a gateway to a whole new way of leading and of being in the world. We've assumed that hierarchy is the only option, because it's the only one we've been trained to recognize as an option. Supposing we want to change the game, we need to recognize that women lead differently, and we also need to unpack what feminine leadership looks like, recognize those behaviors for what they are—leadership—and understand how it creates the power for all of us to lead more effectively in the future.

Putting It to Work

Let's look at an example. Maybe we have a coworker who writes mystery novels in his free time. We can call him Perry. We catch him scribbling during lunch. He is always dressing up as some obscure detective for the fancy-dress office party. He is compelled to write—he can't stop himself! He knows everything there is to know about Tana French and Truman Capote. This impulse, this compulsion, makes him a curious team member. We find him inquisitive by nature, practiced in the game of **perception,** and intently **focused.** Perry writes the best emails. He asks the most unexpected questions. He offers creative ideas for large-scale plans. Perry is a little too focused on his own creativity to excel at the minutiae of operations, but he is a boon, nonetheless. He is a good example of Focused Perception/Strategy—the upper right quadrant of the compass. His interest in mystery novels and his personal practice of expression bring a positive dynamic to his work and nourishes his leadership capabilities. We get a sense of how Perry shows up in the world because of his daily practices.

By now, you have seen examples of healthy and unhealthy leadership traits and qualities at work and in action, and you are more aware of how our environment contributes to them. You can see how they are impacted and sometimes sustained by both the person and the environment or organization in which they work. Most importantly, by now I hope you are beginning to see how we might change environmental factors that amplify the unhealthy traits and qualities. Being seen, heard, and valued are the most fundamental needs for all humans in any society or organization. That's a huge lever for forward progress right there. And you know it exists and are seeing how to use it. Now you can put it into action.

When we put our focus on creating and adopting effective practices, we can seek out new distinctions and build interpretations that push and stretch the common sense of "how things should be done" or "how things are done around here." We can build fresh practices around our new distinctions and interpretations and amplify both our own impact and the impact of the new practices. This leads us to richer conversations, better design, and agile, co-inventive practices.

We follow an evolution of Distinguish → Learn → Do (or Practice and Apply) → Shift Mindset → Behave Differently. It's, of course, not linear, although I've laid it out as if it is here. It's more an evolution, iteration, and recursive process as in the Onboarding New Practices Model.

Onboarding New Practices Model

Behave Differently

Shift Mindset

Do

Learn

Distinguish

- Distinguish: Develop new ideas and language—this is hard and takes time and patience.

- Learn: Onboard the new ideas and distinctions and begin to practice them.

- Do: Develop ways to put this into practice, in the firm belief that it will deliver the results you all seek.

- Shift Mindset: This is the "don't look back; couldn't if I wanted to" moment, where people acknowledge that their worldview has changed so significantly that they never want to go backwards.

- Behave Differently: Once you have shifted your mindset, it's hard or impossible to shift backwards. You can't un-see. With this new mindset, it is inevitable that you will change how you do things—your behaviors. Your team members will do the same and they will want to talk about the shift, the difference, and their new interpretations and perspectives. It is essential to let them do this and to explore this with them as it relates to their work. This is how they truly embody the new effective behaviors. This is where most change initiatives start—trying to change behaviors—and it's why they fail. You can't change behaviors without changing mindsets, unless your people are robots.

Logic, Context, and Feedback

Let's look at an example of a distinction that can lead to learning, doing, shifting mindsets, and behaving differently. Traditional men's leadership emphasizes logic. This style wants things to be linear and step-by-step. Without context and better information-gathering, however, any given series of steps might not turn out to be as logical as they first appear. This is where women's leadership shines. An emphasis on contextualizing is one benefit of this leadership style: accurately perceiving how a project, plan, or specific strategy is interlinked with other problems, issues, opportunities, the customer base, other departments, and/or the wider world. I was watching a TV interview with Jane Fraser, CEO of Citigroup, who said, "Women are better at seeing what I call 'collateral impact.' It makes them very valuable in strategy." Without collateral impact thinking, the most logical plans can create an unforeseen domino effect—a series of problems that quickly escalates and costs time, money, and productivity and can negatively damage any reputation.

Remember when I talked about feedback loops caused by the dominance of one set of traits and assumptions in our environment? Any sort of unconscious pattern can make deliberate progress difficult. The behavior loop discourages others from speaking up and providing input. The team then loses out on opportunities that could save time and money, as well as lead to better outcomes. The masculine emphasis on logic, if used exclusively, creates this kind of feedback loop and shuts out consideration of context. If you've ever found yourself complaining about decisions that seemed to be made in a vacuum, it's because they lacked context. Decisions that seem divorced from context may appear logical to someone, but for someone else who didn't have all the necessary input, these decisions can seem illogical or unworkable.

New practices are required to incorporate context. This new effort demands:

1   Listening

2   Patience to hear the contributor out

3   Acknowledgment of the potential value in the contribution

Taken together, those three actions can shift the existing feedback. We are creating a new feedback loop. When these new practices become the norm, we have a recurrent action-feedback loop that produces different and better outcomes.

Masculine leadership traditionally relies on linear thinking. It follows the step-by-step sequence that seems the most logical. By virtue of being linear, this approach relies on recalling how similar situations have played out in the past. Relying on the past as the basis upon which we create a new plan can limit how we move into the future. It demands a level of predictability that in this century is scarce. The problem is that the future often looks nothing like the past, and the conditions that enabled a past plan to succeed may have completely changed, dooming a repeat of the old plan to failure.

Feminine leadership involves inductive leaps. Far from being some vaguely mystical "women's intuition," these mental leaps are based on observing and factoring in relatedness, synchronicity, inclusion, and context before formulating an approach. The leaps and broader perspective put a plan into a 360-degree, three-dimensional context, anticipating both helpful and harmful ripple effects while looking for natural synergies that promote better outcomes and reduced effort, stress, cost, and time.

When a balanced leader has the patience to hear out and genuinely consider holistic input, the entire organization stands to benefit. Positive acknowledgment encourages more people to look for this sort of synchronicity and to speak up with related ideas. This blending of the best of leadership opens a wider door to ultimately create a healthier work environment for everyone and for better outcomes—not only for employees and stockholders but for consumers, the community, and the world.

Polarization and Exclusion

Blending leadership types and getting holistic input are essential to avoid polarization and exclusion. When exclusively masculine leadership or exclusively feminine leadership prevails—at the cost of balance, wise decision-making, incorporating new perspectives, and powerful convening to listen to and design for the space between—the negative masculine and feminine traits pull in opposite directions.

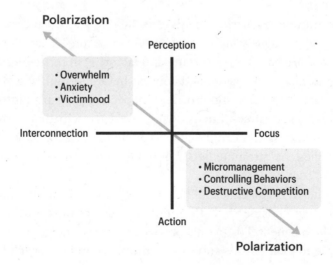

Polarization in Action

When polarization happens in a project, it either expands beyond its effectiveness or collapses in on itself. **Focused action** without any counterbalance can expand beyond its scope and effectiveness. The team loses sight of the customers. The project extrapolates actions beyond their potential value, seeking to "pave the planet" rather than deliver real value. The team loses track of why it exists in the first place. The project becomes its own reason for existence—"tech for the sake of tech." Interconnected perception without any counterbalance can collapse in on itself. The team loses sight of why it exists and who is it there to serve, because it is trying to serve everyone. The project gets stuck and loses direction, focus, and purpose because it is trying to solve for everything, to "boil the ocean."

When this happens, you can:

- Rebalance by looking at the composition of the team to assess if you have the right balance of **focused action** and **interconnected perception** that can create the optimal capacity for strategic and operational excellence.

- Get smart about how the team engages with each other and how the voices on the team are seen, heard, and valued.

- Practice appreciative inquiry—a technique popularized by David Cooperrider and Diana Whitney—which is a very useful practice for bringing out the best in people.

In meetings, polarization happens when people feel isolated and excluded. As a result, they often default to behaviors that can in turn polarize and exclude others. As a leader, it is your job to maximize the value of everyone's time and contribution and facilitate team decision-making in meetings. This becomes difficult or impossible if some individuals are unintentionally polarizing the others. Watch out for:

- Overwhelm: Someone—usually one of your hardest, most generous workers—declares that everyone is moving too fast and then stops contributing.

- Destructive competition: Three guys sit at one end of the conference table and continuously reinforce each other's points, getting louder as the meeting moves ahead.

- Anxiety: Someone is giving all the reasons why others will not like the idea, plan, project, or product.

- Micromanagement: Someone who usually struggles in brainstorming sessions demands to know the details of every next step before anyone can move to the next topic.

When this happens, you can:

- Inquire. Stop the conversation and ask, "What are you seeing there, Ann? How are you seeing that impacting our plan?" Make sure it is not an inquisition but an appreciative inquiry.

- Get smart about your *own* underlying narrative. Make sure you are coming from a place of "I am certain Ann has something wise to say—it just did not click for me" and *not* from "I don't have a clue what she meant, and she is taking up time in my meeting."

- Practice appreciative inquiry.

Compromise Is Scarcity Thinking; Co-invention Is Abundance Thinking

Understand that none of this is about compromise. This is about co-invention and about one of the most powerful aspects of leading from the feminine: leading from wise abundance. Leading from wise abundance is a very powerful strategy for successful leadership. This attitude immediately puts you in "What is possible?" speculation, instead of "Ugh, how do we win the next battle? Climb the next mountain in front of us? Succeed despite the odds?" paranoid scarcity.

Unless the house is on fire, the plane is crashing, or the ship is sinking, leading from wise abundance wins every time. Leading from paranoid scarcity is a state of mind that emerges from fear—of what might happen to us, that we will lose what we do have, and that we will never be able to replace it. One fundamental fear is that there will not be enough to go around.

So how do we, instead, lead from wise abundance? And what does this offer us?

1 Start by asking yourself what you are grateful for. Even with the toughest project, the most challenging problem, the tiniest budget, and the biggest hurdle, there is something to be grateful for. My favorite one is, "I have surrounded myself with great people." Start with that; acknowledge that; build from there.

2 Recognize that leadership is about *much* more than taking action and making money. Leadership, as we usually think of it, is really leadership for creating corporate profit, so that all action must lead to shareholder value—and very little else. We have not looked at leadership as creating a different way of *being* in relation to the world and to each other.

3 Ask yourself and your team how you want to *be* for the duration of the project. What sort of experience do you want to cultivate for you and your people? Do you want to be combative, righteous, critical, overanalytical? If so, then lead from fear and paranoid scarcity. If you want

yourself and your team to be connected, perceptive, focused (in context), creative, and innovative, then you need to lead from wise abundance.

4 Acknowledge that living from wise abundance is the key to amplified leadership. A person who balances their feminine and masculine leadership traits and qualities is on the path to amplified leadership. It is also the key to *being* in the world in a fundamentally different way, one of the keys to leading from wise abundance.

5 Acknowledge that Maslow had a point. When the notorious Abraham Maslow put physiological and safety needs at the bottom of his Hierarchy of Needs, he was gesturing indirectly to the paranoid scarcity mindset. I am certain he never expected us to run our lives, careers, and futures from this place. Many corporations operate from fear and intense competition. As a result, our work environments set us up for just that, every day. But Maslow put self-actualization at the top of his pyramid. You can't self-actualize, be creative, innovate, or have others voluntarily follow you (aka be a real leader) if you still operate from a fear-based, paranoid scarcity mindset.

From here, you have a choice. Do you lead from fear and a mindset of paranoid scarcity? We know this leads to anxiety and overwhelm. It produces 1:1 competition and hyper-control. This is the default assumption we have had for so long—that it's the easy way. Or you can discipline yourself to live in a mindset of wise abundance and invite others to follow you as you nurture a space for creativity, innovation, appreciation, context-creation, and ultimately excellence. You will pleasantly surprise yourself and others, and you will produce much more exciting, sustainable, and valuable results. You may even put yourself on the path to amplifying.

Amplification Creates Value

Amplification happens when we bring, value, leverage, and capitalize on the best of all genders, on the best of the full spectrum of masculine and feminine to the point that you can transcend it and don't even have to pay attention to it. That would be nice!

Let's return again to the 100% Capacity Leadership Compass to see how the combination of healthy masculine and feminine traits and qualities can result in amplification.

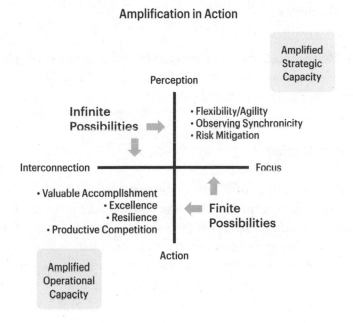

Amplification in Action

We get amplified strategic capacity as evidenced by increased:

- Flexibility
- Agility
- Observation of synchronicity
- Risk mitigation

And we get amplified operational capacity as evidenced by increased:

- Focus on accomplishment and results
- Drive for excellence
- Resilience
- Productive competition

Remember: these are things you have to teach people. These are traits and qualities that come to the table when everyone feels seen, heard, and valued.

Vera's Choice

Vera made her choice. In fact, she made two choices. She chose to accept the job. And she chose to call us in to help. After we worked with Vera's company, her team, and the teams of her male counterparts, Vera confided that we had "taken a weight off her shoulders" and given her a language to easily talk to her male counterparts about something that she had long coped with and skirted around to get by. She had had no language for these conversations without coming across as frustrated and blaming. Similarly, her male counterparts valued Vera but had no clue how she did what she did, and they were frustrated and a bit resentful that they couldn't replicate some of her successes in their own divisions or departments.

Giving them shared language, even though it was clumsy and difficult in the beginning (Vera loved the language, the guys loved the tools and frameworks), somehow cleared the air. They were able to tackle some of the really difficult problems that had been around for a long time and have a bit of a laugh as they were at it. With their help, Vera was able to successfully spearhead the acquisition integration—and get a significant pay raise because it was the "least painful" acquisition in the company's history. She is now head of the acquisition task force, and this is very welcomed by her peers because she "takes the pain out of the process" and instills powerful, innovative processes that make their lives easier and make it easier for them to make their numbers. Thank you, Vera!

6
100% Capacity

Daria, Bob, Evelyn, Tim, and Vera

So how have our five personas been doing? Daria, our director of R&D, reminds me of Purl, the amazing eponymous star of the short movie from Pixar, but at the same time, she has a bit of Seven of Nine about her—the Borg character from *Star Trek: Voyager*, played so magnetically by Jeri Ryan! Ultimately, Daria, like both Purl and Seven, proved that resistance wasn't futile. There are countless other examples I could cite here, and they all relate to the high regard we confer on women who stand up and find the courage to be themselves. Daria achieved this too. Starting small, she brought a team of her peers to a better understanding of how they can lead innovation in a more effective and sustainable way. By focusing on the business value that her pilot project generated, she moved the mountain. The whole way she told the story of gender balance changed; it was a business-focused story, it was powerful, and it produced a massive shift in how the entire corporation innovated and did business.

Bob, the RVP of commercial lending, continued to succeed, and his rate of success accelerated. By engaging more
of his own feminine leadership skills, he started to see how
he could develop much better practices for understanding
his customers and his market, as well as his workforce and
his bosses. He was moved to a much higher role, heading up
one of the largest and most problematic regions for the bank.
Here, he had the opportunity to consciously craft a finely balanced leadership team. Using all he'd learned about creating
a compelling and balanced narrative and focusing on using
speech as a powerful lever to drive change, he turned around
the performance of the region dramatically, and over a three-
year period, it showed sustained improvements in every key
business metric. He had the most fun of his professional life
doing it too.

Armed with a clear set of distinctions around leadership that transcended the traditional output metrics,
Evelyn, head of payment products, was able to put a whole
new structure in place that drove a vastly more collaborative working culture. She was able to call out and examine
exactly what it was that made her business more successful
and use that analysis to give her people the coaching they
needed to engage cross-functionally in a much more effective way. This drove better retention, reduced costs, and
accelerated delivery cycle times. This let Evelyn lift her head
up more often, out of the day-to-day operational challenges
to see bigger strategic opportunities that she could address.
By using tools like the 100% Capacity Maturity Model and
the 100% Capacity Leadrership Compass to determine a
baseline, and by focusing in on the business value exposed
in the Big 7, Evelyn kept on generating transformational
results across her organization.

Tim, CFO of a large multinational, learned from the Six
Lenses for Seeing the Value of How Women Lead and then

followed the Big 7 to catapult from social justice to value generation—and, in doing so, transformed the entire story. This was Tim's big realization, facilitated significantly by the very diverse nature of his role, a CFO to whom all the financial and administrative staff reported. Tim was able to rapidly leverage the HR function to spread the message of gender balance throughout the corporation. For the first time, the team was able to really move the goalposts and change the game! They had the diagnostic skills to identify opportunities to drive actual business results and the tools to drive sustainable change. This shifted their story away from being a cost center that supplied necessary services and towards a new compelling reality where they drove measurable value and were an integral part of the whole company's success.

We have all met a woman like Vera, head of the integration team at the fictional SoBank. Women like Vera can sometimes be intimidating and sometimes very challenging. Their lived experience in the workplace has taught them that a carapace of cynicism and distrust is a survival skill. They lead from a place of scarcity, the logic of quotas has eroded their self-confidence, and they see "more women" as "more competition." Like everyone's, Vera's lens fit her perfectly, but by channeling her immense pride in her work, her strength as a protective leader, her respect for getting the job done right, and her deep appreciation for her customers, she was able to transcend. She became a highly valued member of the C-suite and a powerful force for sustainable change and responsible performance within the company. While many of their competitors were consumed with a "growth at all costs" approach, which exposed their investors to ever-increasing risk, SoBank continued to grow by delivering better—and by acquiring other operators that had imploded when various market events caused their riskier decisions to catch up with the reality of their unsustainable business practices.

A Big Old Call to Action

The last persona I'd like us to spend some time on isn't really a persona; it's a person. It's you.

I find the process of researching, analyzing, and writing personas very cathartic. It's something my team and I do a lot with our clients, sometimes for internal purposes, like ideal candidate profiles, and sometimes to help them understand their customers better. Personally, though, I like to write out my own persona from time to time, to see myself in the third person. What is Jennifer Kenny taking for granted? What assumptions is she making? What limitations is she putting on herself? In my experience, one of the most interesting aspects of this is what it allows me to see not only in myself but in others. It helps me develop greater empathy for those around me, and it makes me significantly more adept in my ability to reach the Darias, Bobs, Evelyns, Tims, and Veras. This goes well beyond the confines of this book, but if you'd like to explore it further, scan the QR code on the Community page at the end of this book to sign up for some tools that can help you work through a persona generation process.

Mobilizing Positive Change: How Would You Like to Transform?

By now, you have probably begun to imagine how this might work in your own organization. What results can you achieve? Who do you need to include? From whom do you need backing or sponsorship? Who are the best people to engage in the design and implementation? We talked about some of the structural aspects of this in chapter 4. Let's look at some guidelines—not just for making it successful but for making it yours.

Start by thinking back to any change or transformation program that you have been involved with. How did you talk about it? How do you refer to it today in terms of the learning you did?

Chances are, if it was successful, you had the following:

1 Speech: how you distinguished or talked about what was valued and practiced by the community. What is your common language? What is the fastest way to build common language with your team and potentially other teams involved in the process? Sustainable, transformational change can't be a top-down, blanket-the-organization thing. You are asking people to change how they think, see the world, speak, and value others. Money can't pay for this. This is discretionary and happens only because someone sees value in it for themselves and the people they care about. They can envision in their mind's eye how this might make things better for themselves and others.

2 Structure: the infrastructure you put in place to support the community (e.g., interest groups, conferences, platforms, analyst organizations). What help can you get? What saves you from doing all the heavy lifting yourself? Are there advisors, conferences, tools, software platforms, etc., out there that can reduce the lift and increase the return? Remember: this is *your* extra discretionary effort. Even if you have been asked to do this by your boss or CEO.

3 Story: how you talked about what was possible.

Keep this as simple and compelling as possible. Pick one and only one area from the Big 7, ideally an area you are personally familiar with. What is the most audacious promise you could make about this area? Who would you make this offer to?

For example, if you and your team are experts at research and development and are therefore primed for pushing innovation, what possibilities can you explore? What specific innovation possibilities are more available to you if you integrate lessons in balanced leadership? We know that mixed-gender teams produce more novel and impactful scientific research. We can take this formula and apply it to our own work. And subsequently we can revise how we talk about what we deliver, as well as expand what we can promise. The stories we tell ourselves and the stories we tell those around us have a tendency to define the outcome. Here, we have a chance to reimagine these stories to the fullest extent. This grants us access to wholly new possibilities.

These are the three major components that need to be in place for any lasting change to happen.

Daria got one of these programs off the ground. She knew firsthand that women led differently, and she'd read the stats on the increased innovation capacity of gender-balanced teams. Over the years, some exceptionally competent male allies had joined her team, and women she had hired around her were simply the best in the business, as were her extended network of women leaders across the business—even if it was a very small network. This felt like betting on herself. And it was something she's always done and benefited from. Daria decided to make an offer to her boss—the division head:

OFFER: I can increase my team's innovation capacity and deliver one more product and two more patents in the next twelve months. This is what the division head is measured on. This offer is supported by a strong business case (*story*) that shows how this is possible and the impact it can have on the division's customer (aka the parent company).

CUSTOMER: Offer made to the division VP.

NEGOTIATE: I can offer to do this *if* HR can bring me a gender-balanced pipeline for my four open positions (*structure*) and I can get help to learn the language and practice of 100% Capacity Leadership (*speech*), establish a learning community, and use the Dynamo platform to accelerate our success (*structure*).

VALUE: Here is what I believe the ROI is on this.

Mobilizing Humans

The most powerful way to effect positive change in any organization is to:

- Help people understand the *solution* differently
- Don't *tell* people what to do differently
- Invite them to see a *better* future for themselves

To do this, we need to help people see what we see, understand why it might matter to them, and realize how it will benefit them. We are asking them to embrace new thinking and put it into practice to produce corporate performance results. We covered this in chapter 5 under the heading "Putting It to Work." This is what you are asking people to do:

- Distinguish: Develop new ideas and language—this is hard and takes time and patience.

- Learn: Onboard the new ideas and distinctions and begin to practice them.

- Do: Develop ways to put this into practice, in the firm belief that it will deliver the results you all seek.

- Shift Mindset: This is the "don't look back; couldn't if I wanted to" moment, where people acknowledge that their worldview has changed so significantly that they never want to go backwards.

- Behave Differently: They will do this themselves. This is where most change initiatives start and also why they fail. People only change because they want to, and when they want to, there is very little anyone can do to stop them. You'd be smart to tap into that force!

Anyone considering an initiative like this always feels alone as they get started. You don't have to feel that way. You are not alone. You are working to mobilize change and create shared purpose and common language, as well as to help people establish a level of competence in something that really matters to them and could transform their lives. It makes sense not to go it alone.

Making the Value Real

Throughout this book, I have shown the path to a strong value proposition. As you complete multiple projects using this approach and methodology:

- You deliver better performance across the Big 7 business imperatives.

- You switch focus to value and contribution.

- This way of working becomes part of the normal business practices and cycles and gets applied to real-world problems and opportunities. It becomes part of the company's toolkit for tackling problems and seeing and realizing opportunities.

- You expand your understanding of the value of our full leadership capacity. You use your existing metrics to determine value and ROI, and you develop more sophisticated metrics to assess your progress and impact.

Over to You!

One of the criticisms I've faced over the years is that I'm not aggressive enough or assertive enough, or maybe somehow, because I'm empathetic, it means I'm weak. I totally rebel against that. I refuse to believe that you cannot be both compassionate and strong.

JACINDA ARDERN, *former prime minister of New Zealand*

New Zealand can justly claim to be the first self-governing country to grant the vote to all adult women. It did so in 1893. Dame Jennifer Mary Shipley became the first woman to be prime minister of New Zealand in 1997, and she held the office for two years. Helen Clark became New Zealand's first elected woman prime minister in November 1999. But neither of these women have the name recognition of New Zealand's fortieth prime minister, Jacinda Ardern, who held the role until January 2023.

At every available point in this book, I've tried to make it as plain as I possibly can that when I talk about the power of gender balance, I'm really not talking about gender. Leadership isn't about gender; it's about power and the ability to inspire and amplify others. However, leadership has been gendered. Unconsciously or consciously, we've been brought up to associate leadership with characteristics that are predominantly masculine in their nature. Given that until 1893, women everywhere were largely deprived of the opportunity to democratically choose our own leaders, this is not too surprising, but as we've explored already, this is a common sense belief that isn't working particularly well for anyone—or at least anyone focused on a longer term than a poor goldfish, trapped endlessly swimming in circles in the same bowl.

Those who don't make an effort to understand history are condemned to repeat it. The painful truth, however, is no one working in a modern company in the twenty-first century has to look any further than their smartphone, or think back any further than their last meeting, to come up with examples of hugely gender-polarizing and ineffective leadership. Its very pervasiveness has a carbon-monoxide-like quality about it, and we've become blind to its effects.

For a very long time, the focus of almost every conversation about gender balance has been about the damage and what we need to do to right the wrongs. By writing this book, it's my most sincere wish that I've made you, and hopefully many others, more aware of the very real and absolutely dazzling opportunity that we have, and that I've provided you with the tools you need to not just start the conversation but to take action.

The next step, which is the most critical one, has to be yours, because only you have the power to take it. I absolutely appreciate that making change happen takes both courage and self-awareness; it's hard. Yet I believe that we can generate the resilient and enduring power we need by reaching inside ourselves and connecting to the feminine essence that has been an integral part of our shared humanity. That power is there. It's beautiful, it's dazzling, it's vast, it's power with and not power over, and it's available to you. Like being compassionate and strong, it's the foundation of balanced leadership, and it exists at the very heart of human endeavor.

With immense love, respect, and gratitude,
Jennifer

Acknowledgments

I AM SO grateful for all the help I have had this year on this book. I've had the pleasure and honor of working alongside brilliant and visionary people: my brother David Kenny, and my daughter, Julia Reichard.

I read *The Goal* by Eliyahu M. Goldratt and Jeff Cox early in my career. I found this book personal and clear-cut. It felt fresh when it came out, and it made an impact on business readers. The book offered me a road map—a way to structure my own ideas about leadership. Between Goldratt and Cox's book and my own ideas, experiences, and research about leadership, I knew that I had something specific to offer. Eventually, my ideas about gender and balanced leadership coalesced with the early business books that had influenced my thinking.

I am extremely grateful to my wonderful clients who have inspired me with their passionate leadership and their driving desire for self-development. I wrote this book for them. Directly or indirectly, each person I have worked with at each client has influenced my thinking. I am grateful for those unique experiences.

Lastly, this book would still be a dream without the support and belief of Trena White, who saw the possibility and stuck with me for three years while I fleshed it out; road tested the research, thinking, frameworks, and assessments; and wrote and published another book on innovation. This book would still be a skeleton draft without the heavy lifting done by James Harbeck and the rest of the team at Page Two. It takes a whole crew of people to publish a book, and I am glad to have had help realizing my vision and very grateful for the welcome they have given me.

Notes

Introduction

p. 5   *an overdose of Iso E Super:* Marin Kristic, "Dior Fahrenheit Review (2023): A Timeless Masterpiece," *Scent Grail*, January 31, 2023, scentgrail.com/holy-grail-scents/dior-fahrenheit-review.

p. 7   *"since the strength of the chain:* Eliyahu M. Goldratt and Jeff Cox, *The Goal: A Process of Ongoing Improvement*, 3rd revised ed. (Great Barrington, MA: North River Press, 2004).

p. 7   *Gender-balanced leadership offers tangible value:* McKinsey Global Institute, *The Power of Parity: How Advancing Women's Equality Can Add $12 Trillion to Global Growth*, September 2015, mckinsey.com.cn/wp-content/uploads/2015/10/MGI-Power-of-parity_Full-report_September-2015.pdf.

p. 9   *"In each of us two powers preside:* Virginia Woolf, *A Room of One's Own* (London: Penguin, 2004), 113–14.

Chapter 1: Double Your Capacity

p. 23   *"the unspoken, unobserved frame of reference:* quotation from Fernando Flores, *Conversations for Action and Collected Essays: Instilling a Culture of Commitment in Working Relationships*, ed. Maria Flores Letelier (self-published, 2012). I was first introduced to Flores's concept of common sense in Terry Winograd and Fernando Flores, *Understanding Computers and Cognition: A New Foundation for Design* (New York: Ablex Publishing, 1986).

p. 26   *76% more likely to get innovative ideas to market:* EY,
          "Could Gender Equality Be the Innovation Boost Utilities
          Need?" March 8, 2019, ey.com/en_ca/women-power-utilities/
          could-gender-equality-be-the-innovation-boost-utilities-need.

p. 26   *Better decisions 73% of the time:* Cloverpop, *Hacking Diversity
          with Inclusive Decision-Making,* n.d., cloverpop.com/hubfs/
          Whitepapers/Cloverpop_Hacking_Diversity_Inclusive_Decision_
          Making_White_Paper.pdf.

p. 26   *24% fewer governance controversies:* Vivian Hunt, Dennis
          Layton, and Sara Prince, "Why Diversity Matters," McKinsey
          & Company, January 1, 2015, mckinsey.com/capabilities/
          people-and-organizational-performance/our-insights/
          why-diversity-matters.

p. 26   *27% more likely to create longer-term customer value:*
          Cristina Milhomem, *Women on Boards: 2020 Progress
          Report,* Morgan Stanley Capital Institute, November
          2020, msci.com/www/women-on-boards-2020/
          women-on-boards-2020-progress/02212172407.

p. 26   *18% higher levels of team commitment:* Julie Sweet and Ellyn
          Shook, *Getting to Equal 2020: The Hidden Value of Culture
          Makers,* Accenture, 2020, accenture.com/_acnmedia/
          Thought-Leadership-Assets/PDF-3/Accenture-Getting-To-
          Equal-2020-Research-Report-IE.pdf.

p. 26   *Two additional percentage points of earnings:* Richard Kersley
          et al., *The CS Gender 3000 in 2019: The Changing Face of
          Companies,* Credit Suisse Research Institute, October 2019,
          credit-suisse.com/media/assets/corporate/docs/about-us/
          research/publications/the-cs-gender-3000-in-2019.pdf.

p. 26   *70% more likely to successfully identify and capture new
          markets:* EY, "Could Gender Equality Be the Innovation
          Boost Utilities Need?"

p. 26   *"Boards with at least 30% women:* EY, "Could Gender Equality
          Be the Innovation Boost Utilities Need?"

p. 27   *"Innovation that uncovers new paths to growth:* EY, "Could
          Gender Equality Be the Innovation Boost Utilities Need?"

p. 27   *"A study by the Center for Talent Innovation:* Sylvia Ann Hewlett
          and Ripa Rashid, *Winning the War for Talent in Emerging
          Markets: Why Women Are the Solution* (Boston: Harvard Business
          Review Press, 2011).

p. 28   *66% higher return on investments:* Marcus Noland, Tyler Moran, and Barbara Kotschwar, "Is Gender Diversity Profitable? Evidence from a Global Survey," Peterson Institute for International Economics, Working Papers 16-3, February 2016, piie.com/publications/working-papers/gender-diversity-profitable-evidence-global-survey.

p. 28   *Women are more likely to seek out additional information:* Vickie Pasterski, Karolina Zwierzynska, and Zachary Estes, "Sex Differences in Semantic Categorization," *Archives of Sexual Behavior* 40, no. 6 (April 2011): 1183–1187, doi.org/10.1007/s10508-011-9764-y.

p. 28   *Women are more likely to engage in collaborative decision-making processes:* McMaster University, "Women Make Better Decisions Than Men, Study Suggests," *ScienceDaily*, March 16, 2013, sciencedaily.com/releases/2013/03/130326101616.htm.

p. 28   *"cooperation, collaboration and consensus-building:* McMaster University, "Women Make Better Decisions."

p. 28   *men were found to be more confident:* Pasterski, Zwierzynska, and Estes, "Sex Differences in Semantic Categorization."

p. 29   *25% lower probability of incurring large financial losses:* Aida Sijamic Wahid, "The Effects and the Mechanisms of Board Gender Diversity: Evidence from Financial Manipulation," *Journal of Business Ethics* 159, no. 3 (2019): 705–725, doi.org/10.1007/s10551-018-3785-6.

p. 29   *higher probability of adopting international financial reporting standards:* Hannu Schadewitz and Jonas Spohr, "Gender Diverse Boards and Goodwill Changes: Association between Accounting Conservatism, Gender and Governance," *Journal of Management and Governance* 26 (September 2022): 757–779, doi.org/10.1007/s10997-021-09607-4.

p. 30   *5.3% increase over the average company:* Hunt, Layton, and Prince, "Why Diversity Matters."

p. 30   *increase overall employee engagement by up to six percentage points:* Kimberly Fitch and Sangeeta Agrawal, "Female Bosses Are More Engaging Than Male Bosses," *Gallup Business Journal*, May 7, 2015, news.gallup.com/businessjournal/183026/female-bosses-engaging-male-bosses.aspx.

p. 30   *gender diversity was positively related to team performance:*
Genevieve Smith, "The Business Case for Gender Diversity,"
International Center for Research on Women, October 2017,
icrw.org/wp-content/uploads/2017/10/Advisors-The-Business-
Case-for-Gender-Diversity.pdf.

p. 30   *gender diversity was positively related to team decision quality:*
Cloverpop, *Hacking Diversity with Inclusive Decision-Making.*

p. 32   *34% higher return on equity:* Noland, Moran, and Kotschwar,
"Is Gender Diversity Profitable?"

p. 35   *Magnet and Charter schools in America have embraced*
mindfulness and meditation: Anya Kamenetz and Meribah
Knight, "Schools Are Embracing Mindfulness, but Practice
Doesn't Always Make Perfect," NPR, February 27, 2020,
npr.org/2020/02/27/804971750/schools-are-embracing-
mindfulness-but-practice-doesnt-always-make-perfect.

Chapter 2: Gender Balance Has Business Value

p. 45   *female representation in senior corporate leadership has grown at*
slightly less than 1%: OECD Analytical Database on Individual
Multinationals and their Affiliates (ADIMA), "What Big Data
Can Tell Us about Women on Boards," OECD, March 2020,
oecd.org/gender/data/what-big-data-can-tell-us-about-women-
on-boards.htm.

p. 45   *start-ups with at least one female founder produce twice the*
revenues and profits: Enterprise Ireland, "Startups Do Better
with Female Founders," 2016, enterprise-ireland.com/en/
funding-supports/Company/HPSU-Funding/NDRC-Do-
Better.pdf.

p. 46   *take 257 years at the current rate of change:* World Economic
Forum, *Global Gender Gap Report 2020*, December 16,
2019, weforum.org/reports/gender-gap-2020-report-100-
years-pay-equality/digest.

p. 46   *66% were feeling pressure from their boards to make diversity and*
inclusion improvements: Mercer, *Let's Get Real about Equality*,
2020, mercer.com/en-us/insights/talent-and-transformation/
diversity-equity-and-inclusion/lets-get-real-about-
equality/#:~:text=When%20Women%20Thrive%20offers%20
an,over%20seven%20million%20employees%20worldwide.

p. 46   *firms were spending eight billion dollars a year on diversity efforts:* Mary Kwak, "The Paradoxical Effects of Diversity," *MIT Sloan Management Review*, April 15, 2003, sloanreview.mit.edu/article/human-resources-the-paradoxical-effects-of-diversity.

p. 47   *Vice President Kamala Harris declared this situation:* Katie Rogers, "2.5 Million Women Left the Work Force during the Pandemic. Harris Sees a 'National Emergency,'" *New York Times*, February 18, 2021, nytimes.com/2021/02/18/us/politics/women-pandemic-harris.html.

Chapter 3: Seeing It in Action

p. 62   *45% of senior women executives leave large corporations:* LinkedIn Economic Graph Team, "Women-Led Businesses Are Growing as Women Leave Workplaces That Aren't Working for Them," LinkedIn, November 18, 2022, economicgraph.linkedin.com/blog/women-led-businesses-are-growing-as-women-leave-workplaces-that-aren-t-working-for-them.

p. 63   *nearly half of all workers (47%) cited work-life balance:* Society for Human Resource Management, "Behavioral Competencies," SHRM (blog), n.d., shrm.org/resourcesandtools/hr-topics/behavioral-competencies/pages/default.aspx.

p. 63   *women are more likely than men to report that their work schedule conflicts:* Erin Rehel and Emily Baxter, "Men, Fathers, and Work-Family Balance," Center for American Progress, February 4, 2015, americanprogress.org/wp-content/uploads/sites/2/2015/02/MenWorkFamily-brief.pdf.

Chapter 4: Engineering New Value

p. 95   *John Gerzema and Michael D'Antonio did some fabulous work:* John Gerzema and Michael D'Antonio, *The Athena Doctrine: How Women (and the Men Who Think Like Them) Will Rule the Future* (San Francisco: Jossey-Bass, 2013).

Chapter 6: 100% Capacity

p. 140 *mixed-gender teams produce more novel and impactful scientific research:* Yang Yang et al., "Gender-Balanced Teams Do Better Work," *Kellogg Insight*, September 13,2022, insight.kellogg.northwestern.edu/article/gender-diversity-successful-teams.

p. 143 *One of the criticisms I've faced:* Maureen Dowd, "Lady of the Rings: Jacinda Rules," *New York Times*, September 8, 2018, nytimes.com/2018/09/08/opinion/sunday/jacinda-ardern-new-zealand-prime-minister.html.

Bibliography

Ahmed, Nafeez. "Patriarchy Is Killing Our Planet—Women Alone Can Save Her." *Ecologist*, March 13, 2015. theecologist.org/2015/mar/13/patriarchy-killing-our-planet-women-alone-can-save-her.

Annis, Barbara, and John Gray. *Work with Me: The 8 Blind Spots between Men and Women in Business.* New York: Palgrave Macmillan, 2013.

"Balance." *The Reluctant Messenger* (blog), n.d. reluctant-messenger.com/balance.htm.

Barnett, Judith, and Jeff Volk. "Corporate Advantage: How Women Leaders Elevate the Bottom Line." U.S. Department of State, Advisory Committee on International Economic Policy, Subcommittee on Women, March 1, 2012. 2009–2017. state.gov/e/eb/rls/othr/2012/184988.htm.

Battah, Pierre. "Early Career Attention Puts Women on Leadership Path." CBC News, April 12, 2015. cbc.ca/news/canada/new-brunswick-early-career-attention-puts-women-on-leadership-path-1.3026622.

Beck, Megan, and Barry Libert. "The Rise of AI Makes Emotional Intelligence More Important." *Harvard Business Review*, February 15, 2017. hbr.org/2017/02the-rise-of-ai-makes-emotional-intelligence-more-important.

Boulton, Clint. "CIOs Walking Digital Tightrope between Opportunity and Risk." CIO, January 17, 2017. cio.com/article/237049/cios-walking-digital-tightrope-between-opportunity-and-risk.html.

Brice, Mattie. "Things I Want the Men in My Life to Know."
 Mattie Brice (blog), August 24, 2015. mattiebrice.com/things-i-want-
 the-men-in-my-life-to-know.

Buckingham, Marcus, and Donald O. Clifton. *Now, Discover Your
 Strengths.* New York: Free Press, 2001.

Bureau for Employers' Activities (ACT/EMP). *The Business Case for
 Change.* International Labour Organization, May 22, 2019.
 ilo.org/global/publications/books/WCMS_700953/lang--en/
 index.htm.

Carroll, Lenedra J. *The Architecture of All Abundance: Creating a
 Successful Life in the Material World.* Novato, CA: New World Library,
 2003.

Catalyst. "Why Diversity and Inclusion Matter (Quick Take)." June 24,
 2020. catalyst.org/research/why-diversity-and-inclusion-matter.

Chormicle, Justin. "Women in Tech: It's Time for
 Change." LinkedIn, April 19, 2017. linkedin.com/pulse/
 women-tech-its-time-change-justin-chormicle.

Cloverpop. *Hacking Diversity with Inclusive Decision-Making.* n.d.
 cloverpop.com/hubfs/Whitepapers/Cloverpop_Hacking_Diversity_
 Inclusive_Decision_Making_White_Paper.pdf.

"Cognitive and Noncognitive Skills." ACT, 2014. act.org/
 content/dam/act/unsecured/documents/WK-Brief-KeyFacts-
 CognitiveandNoncognitiveSkills.pdf.

Condren, Mary. *The Serpent and the Goddess: Women Religion and
 Power in Celtic Ireland.* New York: Harper & Row, 1989.

Conner, Cheryl. "You Can't Have It All: 40% of Women Professionals
 Are 'Hanging On by a Thread.'" *Forbes,* June 8, 2014. forbes.com/
 sites/cherylsnappconner/2014/06/08/you-cant-have-it-all-40-of-
 women-professionals-are-hanging-on-by-a-thread/#5371b42841b9.

Cooperrider, David L., and Diana Whitney. *Appreciative Inquiry:
 A Positive Revolution in Change.* San Francisco: Berrett-Koehler,
 2005.

Copprue, Tanya. *The Secret of the Masculine & Feminine Energies:
 A Guide to Healing Relationships.* Soul De Diva Press, 2010.

Denning, Stephen. *The Leader's Guide to Radical Management:
 Reinventing the Workplace for the 21st Century.* San Francisco:
 Jossey-Bass, 2010.

Desjardins, Jeff. "How Gender Diversity Enhances the Bottom Line."
 Visual Capitalist, January 23, 2018. visualcapitalist.com/
 gender-diversity-bottom-line.

Dowd, Maureen. "Lady of the Rings: Jacinda Rules." *New York Times*, September 8, 2018. nytimes.com/2018/09/08/opinion/sunday/ jacinda-ardern-new-zealand-prime-minister.html.

Eagly, Alice H., Mary C. Johannesen-Schmidt, and Marloes L. van Engen. "Transformational, Transactional, and Laissez-Faire Leadership Styles: A Meta-analysis Comparing Women and Men." *Psychological Bulletin*, 129 no. 4 (July 2003): 569–591. doi.org/10.1037/0033-2909.129.4.569.

Eisler, Riane. *The Chalice & the Blade: Our History, Our Future.* Cambridge, MA: Harper & Row, 1987.

Enterprise Ireland. "Startups Do Better with Female Founders." 2016. enterprise-ireland.com/en/funding-supports/Company/ HPSU-Funding/NDRC-Do-Better.pdf.

EY. "Could Gender Equality Be the Innovation Boost Utilities Need?" March 8, 2019. ey.com/en_ca/women-power-utilities/ could-gender-equality-be-the-innovation-boost-utilities-need.

Ezard, Tracey. "Joy? What's Joy Got to Do with Work?" *Tracey Ezard* (blog), March 13, 2017. traceyezard.com/blog/ joy-what-s-joy-got-to-do-with-work.

Fatemi, Falon. "The Value of Investing in Female Founders." *Forbes*, March 29, 2019. forbes.com/sites/falonfatemi/2019/03/29/ the-value-of-investing-in-female-founders/?sh=34ece81f5ee4.

Fitch, Kimberly, and Sangeeta Agrawal. "Female Bosses Are More Engaging Than Male Bosses." *Gallup Business Journal*, May 7, 2015. news.gallup.com/businessjournal/183026/female-bosses-engaging-male-bosses.aspx.

Florentine, Sharon. "10 Best Places to Work for Women in Technology." CIO, October 12, 2017. cio.com/article/230824/10-best-places-to-work-for-women-in-technology.html.

Flores, Fernando. *Conversations for Action and Collected Essays: Instilling a Culture of Commitment in Working Relationships*, ed. Maria Flores Letelier. Self-published, 2012.

Follett, Mary Parker. *Freedom & Co-ordination: Lectures in Business Organisation.* London, UK: Management Publications Trust, 1949.

Frenier, Carol R. *Business and the Feminine Principle: The Untapped Resource.* San Francisco: New World Library, 1989.

Fusek, Maggie. "'Dear Mr. Google Manifesto': Epic Response from Chemical Engineer, Corp VP, Mom of 5." Patch, August 11, 2017. patch.com/california/mountainview/dear-mr-google-manifesto-epic-response-chemical-engineer-corp-vp-mother-5.

Gawain, Shakti. *The Male and Female Within: Meditations with Shakti Gawain*. Boston: Butterworth-Heinemann, 1997.

Gerzema, John, and Michael D'Antonio. *The Athena Doctrine: How Women (and the Men Who Think Like Them) Will Rule the Future*. San Francisco: Jossey-Bass, 2013.

Goh-Mah, Joy. "Top Ten Books I've Read This Year—A Feminist Perspective." *Media Diversified*, December 26, 2014. mediadiversified.org/2014/12/26/top-ten-books-ive-read-this-year-a-feminist-perspective.

Goldratt, Eliyahu M., and Jeff Cox. *The Goal: A Process of Ongoing Improvement*, 3rd revised ed. Great Barrington, MA: North River Press, 2004.

Hannan, Daniel. "Magna Carta: Eight Centuries of Liberty." *Wall Street Journal*, May 29, 2015. wsj.com/articles/magna-carta-eight-centuries-of-liberty-1432912022.

Harmeyer, Keith. "The Relationship between Creativity and Innovation." LinkedIn, March 2, 2015. linkedin.com/pulse/relationship-between-creativity-innovation-keith-harmeyer.

Harris, Parker. "Salesforce Ranked as #1 Most Innovative Company by Forbes!" Salesforce (blog), August 11, 2017. salesforce.com/content/blogs/us/en/2017/08/salesforce-forbes-most-innovative-2017.html.

Hart, Hilary. *The Unknown She: Eight Faces of an Emerging Consciousness*. Inverness, CA: Golden Sufi Center, 2003.

Helgesen, Sally, and Julie Johnson. *The Female Vision: Women's Real Power at Work*. San Francisco: Berrett-Koehler, 2010.

Hewlett, Sylvia Ann, and Ripa Rashid. *Winning the War for Talent in Emerging Markets: Why Women Are the Solution*. Boston: Harvard Business Review Press, 2011.

Hewlett, Sylvia Ann, Melinda Marshall, and Laura Sherbin. "How Diversity Can Drive Innovation." *Harvard Business Review*, December 2013. hbr.org/2013/12/how-diversity-can-drive-innovation.

Hicks, Marie. "I Gave a Talk at Google and Witnessed a Perfect Example of How Badly Broken the Culture of the Tech Industry Is Today." *Business Insider*, August 11, 2017. businessinsider.com/google-employee-asked-a-surprising-question-during-talk-at-google-uk-2017-8.

Hill, Gareth S. *Masculine and Feminine: The Natural Flow of Opposites in the Psyche*. Boston: Shambhala Publications, 1992.

Hirshman, Linda. "What's the Difference? How Sandra Day O'Connor, Ruth Bader Ginsburg, and Sonia Sotomayor Brought Wisdom to the Supreme Court." *Slate*, August 26, 2015. slate.com/ articles/news_and_politics/jurisprudence/2015/08/how_women_ vote_sandra_day_o_connor_ruth_bader_ginsburg_and_ sonia_sotomayor.html.

Hunt, Vivian, Dennis Layton, Sara Prince. "Why Diversity Matters." McKinsey & Company, January 1, 2015. mckinsey.com/ capabilities/people-and-organizational-performance/our-insights/ why-diversity-matters.

Hunt, Vivian, Sara Prince, Lareina Yee, and Sundiatu Dixon-Fyle. *Delivering through Diversity*. McKinsey & Company, January 2018. mckinsey.com/capabilities/people-and-organizational-performance/our-insights/delivering-through-diversity.

Ivanova, Maria. "Paris Climate Summit: Why More Women Need Seats at the Table." *The Conversation*, November 20, 2015. theconversation.com/paris-climate-summit-why-more-women-need-seats-at-the-table-50116.

Johnson, Allan G. *The Gender Knot: Unraveling Our Patriarchal Legacy*. Revised and updated ed. Temple University Press, 2005.

Joy, Lois, Nancy M. Carter, and Harvey M. Wagner. *The Bottom Line: Corporate Performance and Women's Representation on Boards*. Catalyst, 2007.

Kamenetz, Anya, and Meribah Knight. "Schools Are Embracing Mindfulness, but Practice Doesn't Always Make Perfect." NPR, February 27, 2020. npr.org/2020/02/27/804971750/schools-are-embracing-mindfulness-but-practice-doesnt-always-make-perfect.

Karavitis, Panagiotis, Sotirios Kokas, and Serafeim Tsoukas. "Gender Board Diversity and the Cost of Bank Loans." *Journal of Corporate Finance* 71 (December 2021): 101804. doi.org/10.1016/j.jcorpfin.2020.101804.

Katschilo, Shannon. "Breaking Glass Ceilings Can Lead to a Broken Heart." LinkedIn, September 1, 2015. linkedin.com/pulse/ breaking-glass-ceilings-can-lead-broken-heart-shannon-katschilo.

Kenny, Jennifer. "The Other Lens: The New Essential Leadership Competence." *Women Mean Business*, May 7, 2015. womenmeanbusiness.com/2015/05/the-other-lens-the-new-essential-leadership-competence.

Kersley, Richard, Eugene Klerk, Anais Boussie, Bahar Sezer
Longworth, Joelle Anamootoo Natzkoff, and Darshana Ramji.
The CS Gender 3000 in 2019: The Changing Face of Companies.
Credit Suisse Research Institute, October 2019, credit-suisse.com/
media/assets/corporate/docs/about-us/research/publications/
the-cs-gender-3000-in-2019.pdf.

Kristic, Marin. "Dior Fahrenheit Review (2023): A Timeless
Masterpiece." *Scent Grail*, January 31, 2023. scentgrail.com/
holy-grail-scents/dior-fahrenheit-review.

Kristof, Nicholas D., and Sheryl WuDunn. *Half the Sky: Turning
Oppression Into Opportunity for Women Worldwide.* New York:
Alfred A. Knopf, 2009.

Kuznets, Simon. *National Income, 1929–1932.* Cambridge, MA:
National Bureau of Economic Research, 1934.

Kwak, Mary. "The Paradoxical Effects of Diversity." *MIT Sloan
Management Review*, April 15, 2003. sloanreview.mit.edu/article/
human-resources-the-paradoxical-effects-of-diversity.

Lahiri, Jhumpa. *Interpreter of Maladies: Stories.* London: Flamingo, 2000.

Lakoff, George. "The Women's Marches and the Politics of Care:
The Best Response to Trump's Inaugural Address. " *George Lakoff*
(blog), January 22, 2017.

Landel, Michel. "Gender Balance and the Link to Performance."
McKinsey Quarterly, February 1, 2015. mckinsey.com/
featured-insights/leadership/gender-balance-and-the-link-
to-performance.

Latham, John. *[Re]Create the Organization You Really Want! Leadership
and Organization Design for Sustainable Excellence.* Organization
Design Studio, 2016.

Lean In and McKinsey & Company. *Women in the Workplace 2017.*
wiw-report.s3.amazonaws.com/Women_in_the_Workplace_
2017.pdf.

Lean In and McKinsey & Company. *Women in the Workplace 2019.*
wiw-report.s3.amazonaws.com/Women_in_the_Workplace_2019.pdf.

Lee, Cynthia. "James Damore Has Sued Google. His Infamous
Memo on Women in Tech Is Still Nonsense." *Vox*,
January 8, 2018. vox.com/the-big-idea/2017/8/11/16130452/
google-memo-women-tech-biology-sexism.

Levs, Josh. "How Silicon Valley's Gender Inequality Problem Got
This Bad," *Inc.*, July 11, 2017. inc.com/quora/how-silicon-valleys-
gender-inequality-problem-got-.html.

Libbert, Barry, and Megan Beck. "It's Easier to Replace Leaders
    Than to Reinvent Them." *Forbes*, November 28, 2017. forbes.com/
    sites/barrylibert/2017/11/28/easier-to-replace-leaders-than-
    reinvent-them.
LinkedIn Economic Graph Team. "Women-Led Businesses Are
    Growing as Women Leave Workplaces That Aren't Working for
    Them." LinkedIn, November 18, 2022. economicgraph
    .linkedin.com/blog/women-led-businesses-are-growing-as-women-
    leave-workplaces-that-aren-t-working-for-them.
Ludeman, Kate, and Eddie Erlandson. *Alpha Male Syndrome*. Boston:
    Harvard Business School Press, 2006.
Maslow, Abraham H. "A Theory of Human Motivation." *Psychological
    Review*, 50, no. 4 (1943): 370–396. doi.org/10.1037/h0054346.
McGinty, Emma E., Alene Kennedy-Hendricks, Seema Choksy, and
    Colleen L. Barry. "Trends in News Media Coverage of Mental
    Illness in the United States: 1995–2014." *Health Affairs* 35,
    no. 6 (June 2016): 1121–1129. doi.org/10.1377/hlthaff.2016.0011.
McKinsey Global Institute. *The Power of Parity: How Advancing
    Women's Equality Can Add $12 Trillion to Global Growth*.
    September 2015. mckinsey.com.cn/wp-content/uploads/2015/10/
    MGI-Power-of-parity_Full-report_September-2015.pdf.
McMaster University. "Women Make Better Decisions Than
    Men, Study Suggests." *ScienceDaily*, March 16, 2013.
    sciencedaily.com/releases/2013/03/130326101616.htm.
Meeker, Meg. *Strong Fathers, Strong Daughters: 10 Secrets Every
    Father Should Know*. Washington, DC: Regnery Publishing, 2006.
Mercer. *Let's Get Real about Equality*, 2020. mercer.com/en-us/
    insights/talent-and-transformation/diversity-equity-and-inclusion/
    lets-get-real-about-equality/#:~:text=When%20Women%20Thrive
    %20offers%20an,over%20seven%20million%20employees%
    20worldwide.
Miles, Rosalind. *Who Cooked the Last Supper? The Women's History of
    the World*. New York: Three Rivers, 2001.
Miley, Jeanie. *Joining Forces: Balancing Masculine and Feminine*.
    Macon, GA: Smyth & Helwys Publishing, 2008.
Milhomem, Cristina. *Women on Boards: 2020 Progress Report*.
    Morgan Stanley Capital Institute, November 2020. msci.com/
    www/women-on-boards-2020/women-on-boards-2020-
    progress/02212172407.

Noland, Marcus, Tyler Moran, and Barbara Kotschwar. "Is Gender
Diversity Profitable? Evidence from a Global Survey."
Peterson Institute for International Economics, Working Papers
16-3, February 2016. piie.com/publications/working-papers/
gender-diversity-profitable-evidence-global-survey.

O'Brien, Sarah Ashley. "Biology Isn't Why Tech Is a Boys' Club."
CNN Tech, August 8, 2017. money.cnn.com/2017/08/07/
technology/culture/gender-tech-google/index.html.

Occelli, Cynthia. *Resurrecting Venus: Embrace Your Feminine Power.*
Culver City, CA: Agape Media, 2012.

OECD Analytical Database on Individual Multinationals and their
Affiliates (ADIMA). "What Big Data Can Tell Us about Women on
Boards." OECD, March 2020. oecd.org/gender/data/what-big-
data-can-tell-us-about-women-on-boards.htm.

Owen, Ann L., and Judit Temesvary. "Gender Diversity on Bank Board
of Directors and Performance." *FEDS Notes*. Washington:
Board of Governors of the Federal Reserve System, February 12,
2019. doi.org/10.17016/2380-7172.2270.

Pasterski, Vickie, Karolina Zwierzynska, and Zachary Estes,
"Sex Differences in Semantic Categorization." *Archives of Sexual
Behavior* 40, no. 6 (April 2011): 1183–1187. doi.org/10.1007/
s10508-011-9764-y.

Perry, David M. "What Google Bros Have in Common with
Medieval Beer Bros." *Pacific Standard*, August 22, 2017. psmag.com/
social-justice/alewives-and-google-bros.

Plett, Heather. "What It Means to 'Hold Space' for People, Plus Eight
Tips on How to Do It Well." *Heather Plett* (blog), March 11, 2015.
heatherplett.com/2015/03/hold-space.

Popova, Maria. "Virginia Woolf on Why the Best Mind Is the
Nonbinary Mind." *The Marginalian*, April 15, 2015.
themarginalian.org/2015/04/15/virginia-woolf-androgynous-mind.

Priester, B.J. "The Heroine's Journey: How Campbell's Model Doesn't
Fit." *FANgirl* (blog), April 30, 2012. fangirlblog.com/2012/04/
the-heroines-journey-how-campbells-model-doesnt-fit/.

Rehel, Erin, and Emily Baxter. "Men, Fathers, and Work-Family
Balance." Center for American Progress, February 4, 2015.
americanprogress.org/wp-content/uploads/sites/2/2015/02/
MenWorkFamily-brief.pdf.

Rifkin, Jeremy. *The Empathic Civilization: The Race to Global Consciousness in a World of Crisis*. New York: Penguin/Tarcher, 2009.

Robbins, Cindy. "Equality at Salesforce: The Equal Pay Assessment Update." Salesforce (blog), March 8, 2018.

Rogers, Katie. "2.5 Million Women Left the Work Force during the Pandemic. Harris Sees a 'National Emergency.'" *New York Times*, February 18, 2021. nytimes.com/2021/02/18/us/politics/women-pandemic-harris.html.

Rohn, Jim. "Rohn: 7 Personality Traits of a Great Leader," *Success*, May 3, 2017. success.com/article/rohn-7-personality-traits-of-a-great-leader.

Rowley, Melissa. "What Silicon Valley Can Learn from Lebanon's Women in Tech." *TechCrunch*, June 6, 2017. techcrunch.com/2017/06/06/what-silicon-valley-can-learn-from-lebanons-women-in-tech.

Sandberg, Sheryl. *Lean In: Women, Work, and the Will to Lead*. New York: Alfred A. Knopf, 2013.

Sanford, John A. *The Invisible Partners: How the Male and Female in Each of Us Affects Our Relationships*. New York: Paulist, 1980.

Saunders, Darren. "Confessions of an Overconfident, Mediocre Man." ABC News (Australia), May 27, 2017. abc.net.au/news/2017-05-28/confessions-of-a-confident-mediocre-man/8562708.

Schadewitz, Hannu, and Jonas Spohr. "Gender Diverse Boards and Goodwill Changes: Association between Accounting Conservatism, Gender and Governance." *Journal of Management and Governance* 26 (September 2022): 757–779. doi.org/10.1007/s10997-021-09607-4.

Schwartz, Tony. "New Research: How Employee Engagement Hits the Bottom Line." *Harvard Business Review*, November 8, 2012. hbr.org/2012/11/creating-sustainable-employee.html.

Sherwin, Bob. "Why Women Are More Effective Leaders Than Men." *Business Insider*, January 24, 2014. businessinsider.com/study-women-are-better-leaders-2014-1.

Smith, Genevieve. "The Business Case for Gender Diversity." International Center for Research on Women, October 2017. icrw.org/wp-content/uploads/2017/10/Advisors-The-Business-Case-for-Gender-Diversity.pdf.

Society for Human Resource Management. "Behavioral Competencies." *SHRM* (blog), n.d. shrm.org/resourcesandtools/hr-topics/behavioral-competencies/pages/default.aspx.

Stevens, Heidi. "Why Do Women Get All Attractive If They Don't Want to Be Harassed? Glad You Asked." *Chicago Tribune*, November 2, 2017. chicagotribune.com/lifestyles/stevens/ ct-life-stevens-sunday-why-do-women-make-themselves-attractive-1105-story.html.

Sweet, Julie, and Ellyn Shook. *Getting to Equal 2020: The Hidden Value of Culture Makers*. Accenture, 2020. accenture.com/_acnmedia/ Thought-Leadership-Assets/PDF-3/Accenture-Getting-To-Equal-2020-Research-Report-IE.pdf.

Tarr-Whelan, Linda. *Women Lead the Way: Your Guide to Stepping Up to Leadership and Changing the World*. San Francisco: Berrett-Koehler, 2009.

Teare, Gené. "Global VC Funding to Female Founders Dropped Dramatically This Year." *Crunchbase*, December 21, 2020. news.crunchbase.com/venture/global-vc-funding-to-female-founders.

Thoele, Sue Patton. *The Woman's Book of Soul: Meditations for Courage, Confidence & Spirit*. Berkeley, CA: Conari, 1998.

Toer, Pramoedya Ananta. *This Earth of Mankind*. New York: Penguin Books, 1996.

Turban, Stephen, Dan Wu, and Letian Zhang. "When Gender Diversity Makes Firms More Productive." *Harvard Business Review*, February 11, 2019. hbr.org/2019/02/research-when-gender-diversity-makes-firms-more-productive.

Vernasco, Lucy. "Women Are Poorer Than Men in Every State." *The Daily Beast*, April 14, 2017. thedailybeast.com/ women-are-poorer-than-men-in-every-state.

Vincent, Nora. *Self-Made Man: One Woman's Year Disguised as a Man*. New York: Penguin Books, 2006.

Wahid, Aida Sijamic. "The Effects and the Mechanisms of Board Gender Diversity: Evidence from Financial Manipulation." *Journal of Business Ethics* 159, no. 3 (2019): 705–725. doi.org/10.1007/s10551-018-3785-6.

Wang, Ching-Ching. "Why Blockchain Can Have My Baby." LinkedIn, February 17, 2017. linkedin.com/pulse/ why-blockchain-can-have-my-baby-ching-ching-wang.

Warner, Judith. "Fact Sheet: The Women's Leadership Gap." Center for American Progress, March 7, 2014. americanprogress.org/issues/women/reports/2014/03/ 07/85457/fact-sheet-the-womens-leadership-gap.

"Why Women Are More Generous Decoded." *Tribune India*,
    October 16, 2017. tribuneindia.com/news/science-technology/
    why-women-are-more-generous-decoded/483111.html.

Wiley, Robert W., Colin Wilson, and Brenda Rapp. "The Effects
    of Alphabet and Expertise on Letter Perception." *Journal of
    Experimental Psychology: Human Perception and Performance* 42,
    no. 8 (August 2016): 1186–1203. doi.org/10.1037/xhp0000213.

Williams, Joan C., and Rachel Dempsey. *What Works for Women
    at Work: Four Patterns Working Women Need to Know*. New York:
    New York University Press, 2014.

Windrem, Robert. "Sisterhood of Spies: Women Crack the Code
    at the CIA." NBC News, November 14, 2013. nbcnews.com/news/
    other/sisterhood-spies-women-crack-code-cia-f2D11594601.

Winograd, Terry, and Fernando Flores. *Understanding Computers
    and Cognition: A New Foundation for Design*. New York:
    Ablex Publishing, 1986.

Woolf, Virginia. *A Room of One's Own*. London: Penguin, 2004.

World Economic Forum. *Global Gender Gap Report 2020*. December 16,
    2019. weforum.org/reports/gender-gap-2020-report-100-
    years-pay-equality.

Yang, Yang, Tanya Y. Tian, Teresa Woodruff, Benjamin F. Jones, and
    Brian Uzzi. "Gender-Balanced Teams Do Better Work." *Kellogg
    Insight*, September 13, 2022. insight.kellogg.northwestern.edu/
    article/gender-diversity-successful-teams.

Zmunda, Natalie. "Women Do the Heavy Lifting at Gatorade."
    Ad Age, September 24, 2012. adage.com/article/cmo-interviews/
    women-heavy-lifting-gatorade/237368.

About the Author

JENNIFER KENNY is CEO of jenniferkenny.com and co-founder of 100% Capacity, a SaaS platform that builds market-leading innovation capacity for companies such as Toyota, BlueScope, Wells Fargo, and Woven. Jennifer is a serial entrepreneur who speaks and writes extensively on the topic of building innovation capacity, with a specific focus on two of the big levers of innovation: technology and gender diversity. Her work is founded on Systems Thinking and Language-Action Design/Human-Centered Design. In addition to her books, her work has been featured by Stanford University in its Executive Briefings Program and by Women in Technology International, as well as in *Forbes*, the *San Francisco Business Times*, and *IndustryWeek*, among other publications.

Previously, Jennifer was the CIO of SRI International, where she led the transformation of its information technology organization into a driver of measurable business innovation. She has previously held leadership roles at Webex, Cisco, Wells Fargo, Booz Allen, and Accenture. Jennifer has also served in a number of international academic roles such as advisor to the president of Tanri Abeng University,

Executive Center for Global Leadership, Jakarta; PMO lead at the University of California, San Francisco Medical Center; Featured Entrepreneur at the University of Colorado Boulder Profiles in American Enterprise program; and guest lecturer at the Santa Clara University Leavey School of Business MBA program.

Her previous book, *The Innovation Mindset*, achieved best-seller status across multiple categories, and was described by Dr. Wolfram Burgard (the globally renowned leader in robotics research at the University of Technology Nuremberg) as providing a "unique view into how to improve human collaboration in support of greater innovation."

Jennifer has a master's degree in geotechnical engineering from Imperial College London, a BSc in geology and chemistry from University College Dublin, and postgraduate qualifications from the Stanford Graduate School of Business. She is the past chair of the Global Women's Leadership Network, where she led the receipt of two million dollars in grant funding by the Bill & Melinda Gates Foundation, and is a founding venture partner in How Women Invest.

Engage With Our Innovation Community

THANK YOU FOR READING *100% Capacity*. I hope you found it useful, and I would like to invite you to join one of our Innovation communities. Sign up by scanning the unique QR code below and answering a few questions about yourself.

I MENTION SEVERAL ENGAGEMENTS with clients, all of whom I've worked with through my company, 100% Capacity. We deliver progress with leadership programs that bring 100% Capacity and the Innovation Mindset to life, creating practices that drive sustained success and deliver improved results.

IF YOU WOULD LIKE TO LEARN MORE about these programs or book an in-person conference speech to bring 100% Capacity Leadership to your enterprise, please visit our website at **100capacity.com** or get in touch via email at **info@100capacity.com**. You can also order bulk copies of this book at a discounted rate.